THE END TIMES REVEALED

LIKE NEVER BEFORE

THE OPENING OF END TIME SCRIPTURES REVEALED

FROM GENESIS TO REVELATION

ALAIN DUBREUIL

ISBN- 9798725073164

Because of the dynamic nature of the internet, any web addresses or links contained in this book may have changed since publication and may no longer be valid.

Cover Photo Credit: Jimmy Latreille

All Scripture quoted in this work are from the King James Version (KJV).

PERMISSION GIVEN

I believe this book is going to be **crucial** to those who will have been left behind. Which is why I say to all those reading this before the tribulation has begun, that if you can, send copies to family, friends, and churches. Whether it be in a physical book form, e-book or PDF printed.

You have my permission to get and make copies, but NEVER to make changes to it or make any money from it. Our purpose for placing it on Amazon is for a wider global audience that our ministry on its own may otherwise never have reached. The more people are made aware of this information, the more will be able to prepare themselves and help others.

DEDICATION

First and foremost, not only this book, but also the ministry that began about 3.5 years ago, is dedicated to our Lord and Savior, Jesus Christ, by the will of the Father and the leading of the Holy Spirit. "Use it Lord for Your will. I love You and thank You".

To my very patient, loving and beautiful wife, Winnie, or "Win". We often hear about how the supporting spouse was strong and patient. You absolutely were and are. However, it went beyond just this book to be completed over a period of three weeks, which in itself is incredible. It all goes back to the beginning when we met and were married 20 years ago. You are the love of my life. Within minutes of meeting you for the first time, I knew I was going to marry you. It was most certainly another Spirit-led moment in my life. "Thank you Babe, I love you."

To my two kind, loving and beautiful children in the Lord, my son, Ocean and daughter, Alaina. Thank you for being such good and easy kids. You have not only been a blessing in our lives, but in your goodness have made our job as parents easier. I love you both very much.

To my mother Lise, I love you very much and thank you for everything, especially your prayers. To my sister Mona, I love you and thank you for being there when needed.

A special thanks to my Brother in Christ, Jimmy, without his last minute prompting to get this important book done for the world to have access to, as well as his artistic skills in designing it, it truly would never have happened. The Lord knows we often work better when the pressure is on. This was most certainly demonstrated in having finished everything within three weeks, never having written or designed a book before. Thank you for all the work you did for the Lord on the website as well. It has been a great blessing to tens of thousands of people worldwide. Love you Brother.

To my dear Sister in Christ, Pietra. If it was not for the fact that we knew you were a writer, because of your books we share on the website, I feel we would have been dead in the water upon trying to begin. As you now know, I am a terrible writer, but with your GOD given skills we were able to make this happen. I may know how to say and show the words, but you certainly made them readable for the world. I love you and thank you.

To another Sister in Christ, Tricia. Thank you for your finishing touches to help us get it out to the world as quickly as possible upon completion. The timing was crucial for the time we are in. Much love to you always.

And finally to all you "Fourteeners" around the world. Those I know and those I have never met. You have all had a part in making this happen. Whether in prayers for the ministry, some incredible intercessions along the way, support that helped keep it going, or sharing what you have come to understand in the revelations with others. Thank you all from the bottom of my heart. I love you and pray for you and your families. I look forward to meeting you all very soon. GOD bless.

Sincerely,

Alain Dubreuil

TESTIMONIES

Two years ago when I was supernaturally led to Ministry Revealed, I kept asking the Lord to show me if this was true. Alain teaching's matched over and over again with biblical patterns, types and shadows, and correlations concerning the End Times. For me all these little gears just fell into their grooves. The whole Bible became a dynamic, moving, living story of God's start-to-finish plan with beautiful precision. Everyone needs this revelation as this part of history draws to a close. I pray every reader will set aside that which they think they know and discover a plan for redemption that has existed from the beginning. The wonder of it attests to God's sovereignty, goodness, and glory!

Tricia Exman, PPCC, USA
Tricia Exman Coaching
Living Fearless, Brilliant, Limitless!

> ***Daniel 12:9*** *(KJV)*
> And he said, "Go thy way, Daniel: for the words are closed up and sealed till the time of the end."

For almost 2000 years Christians and biblical scholars have sought to understand the last days and the time of the end. Differences of understanding have driven wedges of division between individuals, churches and denominations, each claiming to have the correct understanding. What they failed to consider is that the books were sealed till the time of the end. That time has now arrived and true to God's Word, the books have been opened, revealing the truth of exactly what is about to transpire. For reasons beyond our understanding, the Lord God has chosen and called Alain Dubreuil of Ministry Revealed, as well as many faithful brothers and sisters in Christ, to open the books and reveal the keys to understanding the End Times that are now upon us.

You will find these keys to understand the revelations in this book to be proven directly from the scriptures and will show you the Word of God has a "WAS", an "IS", and an "IS TO COME" aspect to be understood. Further proving that the End Time prophecies and Gods plan for the redemption of man are written in the Law, in the Psalms and in the Prophets (Luke 24:44).

Without a doubt, this book will prove to be an essential resource that you will find indispensable and an aid through your tests and trials. In the midst of confusion and perplexity, you will gain understanding, hope and strength knowing that our Lord has been, and remains in total control of ALL that transpires in heaven and on earth.

Ask the Lord Jesus to make this revelation, YOUR REVELATION.

Ivan Stouffs, South Africa
Entrepreneur

The Holy Spirit led me to Ministry Revealed back in 2017. The key of who the gospels are speaking to and the truth of the tribulation period, have helped open my understanding and has changed the way I see scripture. I now see with “End Time eyes” and the Word rings true in my spirit. Before Ministry Revealed, I had too many questions and not enough answers. The keys given in Ministry Revealed have undeniably answered many of those questions. The Lord has blessed this ministry with revelation upon revelation and the books have been opened. It has been an amazing journey. 5 STARS!

Tabby Bizgan, USA
Adult Care Facility Owner/Provider

As a Christian most of my life, I never had a good understanding of End Times. Maybe a little here and there. I knew about a 7 year tribulation and the rapture of the church. When I was told of the Revelation 12 sign that happened on the 23rd September 2017, I wanted to know more and prayed for guidance. A year went by without anything happening, nothing changed. And then one day I heard this voice say "Hello Fourteeners! Welcome back to Ministry Revealed!" From that moment my whole life changed. You have to read this book! It is amazing and the best thing is, it is all true! So keep an open mind. There is a good chance your life will be changed too.

Neal Page, USA
Carpenter

Table of Contents

INTRODUCTION.....1

A NEW JOURNEY OF REVELATION.....1

CHAPTER 1.....6

WHO THE GOSPELS ARE SPEAKING TO.....6

A BRIEF SUMMARY OF THE GOSPELS OF LUKE, MARK, AND MATTHEW.....7

LUKE.....7

MARK.....8

MATTHEW.....8

REDEMPTION, TRIBULATION AND GREAT TRIBULATION IN SCRIPTURE.....11

REDEMPTION.....11

TRIBULATION.....13

GREAT TRIBULATION.....14

REVEALED IN THE ROBE: JESUS' GARMENT DURING THE CRUCIFIXION.....15

LUKE.....16

MARK.....16

MATTHEW.....16

JOHN.....17

THE FINAL WORDS SPOKEN BY JESUS ON THE CROSS: "MY GOD, MY GOD, WHY HAST THOU FORSAKEN ME?".....18

LUKE.....19

MARK.....19

MATTHEW ... 19
THE FINAL INSTRUCTIONS GIVEN BY JESUS ... 20
"CARRIED UP / RECEIVED UP / RETURNED AND STAYING" ... 23
CARRIED UP ... 23
RECEIVED UP ... 24
RETURNED and STAYING ... 24
THE ABOMINATION OF DESOLATION (SPOKEN OF BY DANIEL THE PROPHET) ... 25
THE SIGN OF JONAH IS NOT THE SAME IN EACH GOSPEL ... 31
THE 40 DAYS WARNING (in Luke) ... 31
NO SIGN (in Mark) ... 33
3 DAYS AND 3 NIGHTS (in Matthew) ... 37
PREPARING THE PASSOVER ... 40
GOD'S HARVEST MODEL ... 47
CHAPTER 2 ... 51
WHEN THE YEARS JUST DON'T ADD UP ... 51
FOURTEEN YEARS SPOKEN OF BY PAUL ... 51
THE FIRST GROUP - LUKE / BRIDE ... 52
THE SECOND GROUP - MARK / LEFT BEHIND ... 53
THE THIRD GROUP - MATTHEW / JEWS ... 55
ON THE MOUNT OF TRANSFIGURATION ... 56
THE BIG PICTURE GIVEN IN THE STORY OF JACOB ... 60
CHAPTER 3 ... 65
THE 40 DAYS OF THE SON OF MAN ... 65
WHAT SIGN IS "JONAH" AND WHEN? ... 68

LUKE 69
MARK 69
MATTHEW....69
THE RESURRECTION 82
LUKE 82
MARK 82
MATTHEW....83
A WORD OF CAUTION (THAT GIVES GREATER EVIDENCE).....83
PSALM 38 87
CHAPTER 4 89
THE REVELATION OF DANIEL 9 89
CHAPTER 5 110
THE DIFFERENCES AND THE TRUTH 110
CHAPTER 6 125
THE END TIME 7 CHURCHES 125
SEVEN STAGES OF CHURCH HISTORY 127
THE CHURCH OF EPHESUS 129
THE CHURCH OF SMYRNA....130
THE CHURCH OF PERGAMUM....132
THE CHURCH OF THYATIRA....134
THE CHURCH OF SARDIS. 136
THE CHURCH OF PHILADELPHIA 138
THE CHURCH OF LAODICEA 140
CHAPTER 7 145
THE BOOKS HAVE OPENED 145

CHAPTER 8 182

REVEALING REVELATION 182

THE SEALS JUDGMENT 182

WHAT WAS, SHALL BE AGAIN 188

THE TRUMPETS JUDGMENT 209

CHAPTER 9 230

SEEING OR ENTERING THE KINGDOM 230

YOU MUST BE BORN AGAIN 231

YOU MUST BE BAPTIZED 241

HOW BAPTISM RELATES TO JESUS 249

IN WHOSE NAME? 250

RECEIVE THE HOLY SPIRIT 257

APPENDIX 267

REVELATION 22 272

INTRODUCTION

A NEW JOURNEY OF REVELATION

Prior to the Spring of 2017 I had not yet made any videos. And from that point to when everything changed, I had only made a few that were simply from a desire to be part of doing something for the Kingdom of GOD. To hopefully help others come to know our Lord and Savior. But where this ministry officially started for me, was on September 8, 2017.

It was during a video I was making when the Spirit arrested my attention with some scriptures that made me question my End Time understanding. On that day everything changed and a whole new journey of revelation followed. Once I finished that video, things started to slot in their proper place and that which did not make sense before, started to make perfect sense.

Scriptures, never before truly understood in relation to the End Time understanding, began to reveal themselves to me, just as Daniel 12:4 said would happen... that the books were sealed until the time of the End. I can now say, the books have Opened! Scripture after scripture with answers to questions I did not even know were questions! Right from Genesis to Revelation and it kept on revealing the end-time plan and the glory of God. This truly is a revealing ministry by the grace of God and all the glory and honor goes to the Most High God. I would like to mention that all scriptures quoted in this book are the King James Version (KJV).

Now, let me begin with what I am going to call a "statement of understanding". And the reason for it is important. It is the understanding of the 70th year!

You are going to see it mentioned on many pages throughout this book. Not because of the same verse being repeated over and over, but because it is everywhere in scripture when talking about the End Times. For a very long time there had been teachings about when the 70 years of Israel would come, the End Times would be upon the world. But the 70th year according to most biblical scholars' understanding, has come and gone. It is believed by the world to have been from May 2018. And yet nothing had yet begun that whole year?

> ***Daniel 9:2*** *(KJV)*
> **2** In the first year of his reign I Daniel understood by books the number of the years, whereof the word of the Lord came to Jeremiah the prophet, that he would accomplish **seventy years** in the desolations of Jerusalem
>
> ***2 Chronicles 36:21*** *(KJV)*
> **1** To fulfil the word of the LORD by the mouth of Jeremiah, until the land had enjoyed her sabbaths: for as long as she lay desolate she kept sabbath, to fulfil **threescore and ten years**.

However, the Lord's counting is not our counting when it comes to His land. There has been a very important piece of scripture that has been missed by just about all who have taught on End Times and is the reason none of them mention the importance of the 70th year in their talks anymore. They have not yet understood how the LORD GOD counts it. But He does tell us:

> ***Leviticus 19:23-24*** *(KJV)*
> **23** And when ye shall come into the land, and shall
> have planted all manner of trees for food, then ye
> shall count the fruit thereof as uncircumcised: **three**
> **years** shall it be as uncircumcised unto you: it shall
> not be eaten of.
> **24** But in the fourth year all the fruit thereof shall
> be holy to praise the LORD withal.

This is telling us that the LORD had instructed them on how to proceed once they came into the land. Well, we all know they had been removed from the land for almost 2000 years and came into the land again in May 1948. So if for "three years" they were not to take from the land and it was not until the fourth year that it was acceptable to the LORD, what year would that put the 70th in? 1948 + 73 years = 2021

As ***Proverbs 25: 2*** *(KJV)* says:

> *It is the glory of God to conceal a thing, but the honor of kings is to search out a matter.*

I would like to start with a prayer for the readers of this book before we embark on this journey together. This book is not just for the purpose of informing you of the things that you can expect to happen in their seasons, but also about knowing that there is a hope even in the midst of tribulation. God is using this time as a judgment on the sleeping Church and the world, to bring them back to Him because of His desire for all His children to come home. And because He is holy, He expects us to live in obedience to Him and to love Him with all our heart, mind and strength. And to love our neighbors as ourselves. Sadly, as quoted, "*It sometimes takes tribulation for the church to be the church as God intended*". If you are one of those left behind, know that it is often in His judgment that He extends His mercy. When you call out to Him, He promised that He will hear your cry and answer you. This book will also, when given to others to read, wake up the church not only to the judgment on sin and this world, but also to let them know that He will be back to gather His children and that they should have their garments ready. I encourage you to share this book as much as possible.

Father, I ask and pray that the anointing of Your Spirit will be on each reader and all who will hear the words being taught. That You will give them wisdom, knowledge, understanding and discernment. Let them know that this book is a gift, because of your mercy and love for them. Let the truth of the Lord's End Time words being revealed in this book, be received as a blessing in love. I pray that they will search your Word and not be quick to dismiss what is written. You promised that Your Spirit will guide them in all truth and that He will remind them of all Jesus has said. Thank You that You will do this for them. I pray that You will lift the veil from their understanding, with hearts ready to receive that which you personally want to reveal to them, not just about the End Times which is also You, but about all of You. Because to know You is Eternal Life. May they see You in the pages, and be drawn closer to You. Amen.

**This book has been designed to allow you space to make notes as you study...because you'll need it!*

CHAPTER 1

WHO THE GOSPELS ARE SPEAKING TO

In this chapter we will show the comparisons between each Gospel to give the supporting evidence of the truth being revealed. The introduction to who the Gospels are speaking to was the first great revelation that began on September 8, 2017, and it has continued to reveal itself ever since. You will begin to understand, once and for all, the mystery of who the synoptic gospels truly speak to in the End Times and why it matters more than ever, especially in this present time. Having been taught the End Times from mainly the gospel of Matthew's perspective has unfortunately hindered our greater understanding of the End of Days. Causing us to have literally missed half of the tribulation time frame.

As you read the first three gospels, you will likely see countless similarities. However, a closer reading reveals some differences in the details. Are these differences the same as contradictions? And what would be the reason for them being there? Are the Gospels reliable if certain details are different from each other? God's Word is perfect, there can be no contradiction. God cannot lie. Everything the scriptures say is completely true. While Christians recognize this truth, we also understand that if you put the four Gospels side by side, you would discover incongruities, which we cannot deny. A perceptive reader might ask, "What is going on here? Did it happen that way or that way?" The reason for the differences and apparent contradictions are in fact that the synoptic gospels are speaking to different people groups.

A BRIEF SUMMARY OF THE GOSPELS OF LUKE, MARK, AND MATTHEW

LUKE

The Gospel of Luke, or simply Luke, tells of the origins, birth, ministry, death, resurrection, and ascension of Jesus Christ. Together with the Acts of the Apostles, it makes up a two-volume work which scholars call Luke–Acts and together they account for 27.5% of the New Testament. Most modern scholars agree that the traditional view is that it was Luke, the Evangelist and companion of Paul who was the author of the Gospel of Luke. Written to a Greek-speaking audience, but directing his attention specifically to Christian concerns rather than to the Greco-Roman world at large.

A very important verse is found in the 3rd verse of the first chapter that lays the foundation of the importance of why the Gospel of Luke is so important.

> ***Luke 1:3*** *(KJV)*
> It seemed good to me also, **having had perfect understanding of all things** from the very first, **to write unto thee in order**, most excellent Theophilus.

This verse states that Luke had perfect understanding, which I am sure you will agree, is quite a bold statement. He also says that he is writing in order. This should cause us to take note of what is said, and in what order.

MARK

The Gospel of Mark is the second of the four canonical gospels and of the three synoptic gospels. Mark was the companion of the Apostle Peter. Most scholars date it to just after 70 CE, when Titus (a Roman general and subsequently emperor) destroyed the temple. It was written in Greek, for a Gentile audience. Written to strengthen the faith of those who already believed, not to convert unbelievers.

MATTHEW

The Gospel of Matthew is the first book of the New Testament. Matthew seems to emphasize that the Jewish tradition should not be lost in a church that was increasingly becoming gentile. He wrote his gospel to convince fellow Jews that Jesus was the Messiah foretold in the Old Testament. Written from a Jewish viewpoint for a Jewish audience. The internal evidence of this is so overwhelming that it is often called "The Gospel for the Jews." It uses the distinctly Hebraic formula "Kingdom of Heaven", where the other books in the New Testament speak only of the "Kingdom of God".

It is very important to note that even though the gospel of Matthew was written for the Jews, almost all the pastors base their theology and eschatology on the gospel of Matthew, leaving out of consideration the role the gospels of Mark and Luke play. Almost as if they have no real relevance to the End Times and are more like a side note. But in actual fact, taking all the synoptic gospels into consideration makes all the difference to our End Time understanding.

This is probably a good scripture to start this off with –

> ***Matthew 20:16*** *(KJV)*
> So the last shall be first, and the first last. For many be called, but few chosen.

This is literally letting us know that in the end, those who were first shall be last and those who were last shall be first. So with this in mind, out of the synoptic gospels who would then be first? Luke, followed by Mark and finally Matthew. Without trying to say too much here and causing you to scratch your head with questions before we even begin, let me explain it in one simple sentence so that you begin to get into the mindset of the revelation. And then let all the evidence that follows prove it to you.

Luke was written to the Gentile Bride, Mark to the Left Behind Church, and Matthew to the Jews.

With that in mind you will now begin to understand what follows and see how Luke's group is removed before the tribulation even begins. Leaving both Mark and Matthew's groups, as you will see, to endure "portions" of the tribulation. This brings us back to what I said a moment ago, how having been taught from Matthew's point of view for the End Times, has caused half of the tribulation to be missed in its understanding.

Isaiah 46:10 *(KJV)*
Declaring the end from the beginning, and from ancient times the things that are not yet done.

I debated whether I should put this next piece right here at the start or not. But, as you can see, I did. And the reason I did, was to again help set your thoughts for the revelation of these gospels you are about to understand. Because with just about everyone who is going to be reading this, it will be the first time, after a lifetime of having been taught everything from Matthew's perspective. Matthew comes last, not first. This means that you have, without knowing it, been taught the End Times from the end!

I promise you, that what you are about to understand here in this book and especially from this chapter, is going to reveal to you mysteries of the End Times that you have been trying to understand for a very long time. Questions will be answered, and even if not all your questions are answered, you will now have understanding to seek them out yourself.

And this is to whom the gospels are speaking:

Luke
Escape of the Bride of Christ / Pre-Trib / Before the Seals Begin.

Mark
Rapture of the Left Behind / Great Multitude / Mid-Trib / End of Seals

Matthew
Second coming / Jews / Post-Trib / Jacob's Trouble - Trumpets

REDEMPTION, TRIBULATION AND GREAT TRIBULATION IN SCRIPTURE

The Word of God is full of clues that we often miss, especially if we do not know even where to begin. But Father has provided various means to search out His word and individual words much easier now by means of the internet. The blueletterbible.org site and e-sword free app are very good sources to grasp a deeper understanding of what individual words mean with the use of the Strong's Concordance word definitions and to get a panoramic view of scripture. In these studies you will see how great these tools have been in helping us reveal, in many cases, what a word actually means, especially compared to what we simply thought it meant as we read it.

Let's get started with these important words: Redemption, Salvation, Tribulation and Great Tribulation and see specifically where they are used in relation to the three synoptic gospels, which is the focus of this chapter.

REDEMPTION

Redemption is G629, which means ransom in full, that is, (figuratively) riddance, or (specifically) Christian salvation: - deliverance, redemption

When you search the word "Redemption" (G629) (or Redeemed G3085), as well as the word "Salvation (G4991), you will see that it is found only in the Gospel of Luke and not even once in Mark or Matthew.

Luke 21:28 *(KJV)*
And when these things begin to come to pass, then look up, and lift up your heads; for your redemption (G629) draweth nigh.

Romans 8:23 *(KJV)*
And not only they, but ourselves also, which have the firstfruits of the Spirit, even we ourselves groan within ourselves, waiting for the adoption, to wit, the redemption (G629) of our body.

Those with the "firstfruits" of the Spirit are the Bride of Christ, she is the firstfruits of the wheat harvest of the feasts of weeks.

Luke 1:68 *(KJV)*
Blessed be the Lord God of Israel; for he hath visited and redeemed (G3085) his people,

Luke 2:38 *(KJV)*
And she coming in that instant gave thanks likewise unto the Lord, and spake of him to all them that looked for redemption (G3085) in Jerusalem.

Luke 1:69 *(KJV)*
And hath raised up an horn of salvation (G4991) for us in the house of his servant David

Luke 1:71 *(KJV)*
That we should be saved (G4991) from our enemies, and from the hand of all that hate us.

Luke 1:77 *(KJV)*
To give knowledge of salvation (G4991) unto his people by the remission of their sins.

Not one word in the Bible is placed there by accident or for no reason. There is a reason why the words Redemption and Salvation are not found in Mark and Matthew. And the reason for this is that it shows us that the Bride (LUKE) will be redeemed from what is to come, whereas the Left Behind Church (MARK) and Jews (MATTHEW) will have to face tribulation.

TRIBULATION

Tribulation (G2347) means tribulation, affliction, trouble, anguish, persecution, burdened, and to be afflicted (with G1519).

When you search the word "Tribulation" (G2347) on blueletterbible.org it appears in the Olivet discourses of Mark and Matthew. And the Olivet discourses, which are only found in the synoptic gospels, are the literal conversations about the End Times that Jesus had with His disciples after they had asked Him about what the signs of His coming would be. However, not only is this word not found in Luke's Olivet discourse, it is not found anywhere in Luke's gospel!

Mark 13:19 *(KJV)*
For in those days shall be **affliction (G2347)**, such

as was not from the beginning of the creation which God created unto this time, neither shall be.

Mark 13:24 *(KJV)*
But in those days, after that **tribulation (G2347)**, the sun shall be darkened, and the moon shall not give her light

Matthew 24:9 *(KJV)*
Then shall they deliver you up to be **afflicted (G2347)**, and shall kill you: and ye shall be hated of all nations for my name's sake.

Matthew 24:29 *(KJV)*
Immediately after the **tribulation (2347)** of those days shall the sun be darkened, and the moon shall not give her light, and the stars shall fall from heaven, and the powers of the heavens shall be shaken:

GREAT TRIBULATION

And the term "great tribulation" is only found once anywhere in any gospel.

Matthew 24:21 *(KJV)*
For then shall be **great tribulation (G2347)**, such as was not since the beginning of the world to this time, no, nor ever shall be.

The word "**Tribulation"** in Mark is a representation during the years of Seals and the term "**Great Tribulation**" only in Matthew, is represented during the years of Trumpets. Or as many have come to know it, Jacob's Trouble.

In conclusion, the words "Redemption, Redeemed and Salvation" are found only in the synoptic Gospel of Luke. While the words "Tribulation and Great Tribulation" are found in both Mark and Matthew. This begins to shed a little light that there appears to be something more going on with the gospels and that they may be written to different people groups. So hold on tight, because from here on it really gets detailed and interesting.

REVEALED IN THE ROBE:

JESUS' GARMENT DURING THE CRUCIFIXION

This is one of my favorites. Many of us have used this one as a way to bring up in conversation with other believers regarding the revelation of who the gospels are speaking to. It was something that had essentially gone unnoticed or certainly put on the back shelf, because it was not understood. I know I had never heard of a single conversation about it, until we saw it. In fact many here part of the online ministry had asked their pastors about it and not one could answer them. In fact, I do not even recall hearing of one that had even noticed in their 20, 30 and some even in their 40 years of ministry, that there even were different colors.

You will see it right away once it is brought to your attention. But there is even more revealed to us, again in the description of the meaning of the word, for each color. You are about to understand that those colors are very descriptive as to who the gospels are speaking to.

LUKE

Luke 23:11 *(KJV)*
And Herod with his men of war set him at nought, and mocked him, and arrayed him in a **gorgeous (G2986)** robe, and sent him again to Pilate.

Gorgeous G2986 means; radiant; by analogy limpid; figuratively magnificent or sumptuous (in appearance): - bright, clear , gay, goodly, gorgeous, white

Notice that it is white, in the same way that we expect a wedding dress to be. "White" also happens to be the meaning of the name LUKE (G3022) λευκός leukos lyoo-kos' from λύκη lukē ("light"); white: - white

MARK

Mark 15:17 *(KJV)*
And they clothed him with **purple (G4209)**, and platted a crown of thorns, and put it about his head.

Purple G4209 is of Latin origin; the "purple" mussel, that is, (by implication) the red blue color itself, and finally, a garment dyed with it: - purple

As a side note, when we fall or have been hit or run into something, we get bruised and it turns a red blue color or purple, and it leaves a MARK.

MATTHEW

Matthew 27:28 *(KJV)*
And they stripped him, and put on him a **scarlet (G2847)** robe.

Scarlet G2847 is from G2848 (from the kernel shape of the insect); crimson colored: - scarlet (colour, coloured)

Now as much as I said this is about the synoptic gospels of Luke, Mark, and Matthew, this time there is an exception. And that is because John's gospel reveals a great piece of revelation for the End Times as well.

JOHN

> ***John 19:5*** *(KJV)*
> And the soldiers platted a crown of thorns, and put it on his head, and they put on him a **purple (G4210)** robe. And Pilate saith unto them, Behold the man!

Purple G4210 is from G4209; purpureal, that is, bluish red: - purple.

This purple (G4210) in John is different from the purple (G4209) in Mark. But what makes this so amazing is we see that the purple G4210 of John "comes from" the purple G4209 of Mark. And what makes that so interesting you ask?

In Revelation 7 after the Seal judgments from chapter 6, the 144,000 are being sealed. They "come from" the group that is about to get raptured right after them, in the same chapter. And that group, as I explained earlier, is the great multitude. They are the rapture group of Mark at the time of the end of Seals. Hence the representation of John here in this type and shadow being revealed in the robes, as those having been chosen out of Mark to work during the following time of Trumpets, the 144,000.

Let's bring this to a close by getting back to the purple (G4209) color of MARK and the scarlet (G2847) color of MATTHEW. As we read the book of Revelation, we see the very same colors found during the tribulation period of Seals and Trumpets in the following scripture, further proving that these people groups will be here during the tribulation, but again, not the gorgeous (G2986) of the Bride of Christ represented in LUKE.

> ***Revelation 17:4*** *(KJV)*
> And the woman was arrayed in **purple** (G4209) and **scarlet** (G2847), and decked with gold and precious stones and pearls, having a golden cup in her hand full of abominations and filthiness of her fornication.

The "Gorgeous, white" color of Jesus' robe in the gospel of Luke is not found in the tribulation.

With the evidence thus far it is clear that both the people groups of Mark and Matthew will be here during the tribulation.

THE FINAL WORDS SPOKEN BY JESUS ON THE CROSS:
"MY GOD, MY GOD, WHY HAST THOU FORSAKEN ME?"

We all know the well-known last words of Jesus on the cross, "My God, my God, why hast Thou forsaken Me?" But did you know that the word "forsaken" means "left behind"? Once again you will find the contrast in the three synoptic gospels that shows the distinction of the three people groups of LUKE, MARK and MATTHEW.

LUKE

> ***Luke 23:46*** *(KJV)*
> And when Jesus had cried with a loud voice, he said, Father, into thy hands I **commend (G3908)** my spirit and having said thus, he gave up the ghost.

Jesus commended (G3908) His spirit in Luke's account, which means; to place alongside.

MARK

> ***Mark 15:34*** *(KJV)*
> And at the ninth hour Jesus cried with a loud voice, saying, Eloi, Eloi, lama sabachthani? Which is, being interpreted, My God, my God, why hast thou **forsaken (G1459)** me?

MATTHEW

> ***Matthew 27:46*** *(KJV)*
> And about the ninth hour Jesus cried with a loud voice, saying, Eli, Eli, lama sabachthani? that is to say, My God, my God, why hast thou **forsaken (G1459)** me?

Forsaken G1459 is from G1722 and G2641; to leave behind.

In both Mark and Matthew, Jesus cries out, "Father why have you left me behind?" Was Jesus left behind? No! So what was the purpose of Him crying out "left behind" in those two accounts, but yet again, not in Luke's? It clearly was not for Him.

And of course in Luke, the representation of the Bride of Christ, Jesus says, "Father, place me along your side!"

This revelation is clear and easy to grasp.

So what picture are we seeing to this point? The Gentile Bride who is dearly loved and ready with her gorgeous white robe, to be placed alongside the Bridegroom as one would do for a wedding. And Mark and Matthew's groups are being left behind to endure their portions of judgment during the Seals and Trumpets. Not because they have been cast away, but because they were not ready and watching for the Bridegroom. With one last effort, the Lord in His great mercy and love for all, will use this time to wake up those left behind. So that they may understand and realize that without Him there is nothing that can save them. That they will fall on their knees and cry out to Jesus as their Lord and Savior before it is too late.

THE FINAL INSTRUCTIONS GIVEN BY JESUS

Jesus' final instructions to His disciples to go out and do is found in the last chapter of each gospel. There is a lot of great detail in these last chapters that reveal a lot more than what I am relaying here. However, I will go into this in a bit more detail in a later chapter. It is a great revelation and will be worth waiting for. This revelation will once again make the point of who the gospels are speaking to.

We see in the gospels of Luke and Mark that He is instructing His disciples to go out and "preach". However, in Matthew we see He does not instruct them to preach, but to "teach". There is a reason for this difference and it is once again revealed in the End Time understanding.

Luke 24:47-49 *(KJV)*
47 And that repentance and remission of sins should be **preached (G2784)** in his name among all nations, beginning at Jerusalem.

Mark 16:15-16 and 20 *(KJV)*
15 And he said unto them, Go ye into all the world, and **preach (G2784)** the gospel to every creature.
16 He that believeth and is baptized shall be saved; but he that believeth not shall be damned.
20 And they went forth, and **preached (2784)** everywhere, the Lord working with them, and confirming the word with signs following. Amen.

Matthew 28:18 - 20 *(KJV)*
18 And Jesus came and spoke unto them, saying, All power is given unto me in heaven and on earth.
19 Go ye therefore, and **teach (G3100)** all nations, baptizing them in the name of the Father, and of the Son, and of the Holy Ghost:
20 **Teaching (G1321)** them ***to observe*** all things whatsoever I have commanded you: and, lo, *I am with you always*, **even unto the end of the world**. Amen.

The word in Luke and Mark is:

Preach-ed (G2784) to herald (as a public crier), especially divine truth (the gospel): - preach (-er), proclaim, publish. This means to proclaim, preach the gospel, which means go and tell everyone about the saving gospel of Jesus Christ.

However, in Matthew we have a very different story. He does not tell them to go out and preach, but to go and "teach" the world whatsoever He has commanded them.

Teach (G3100) intransitively to become a pupil; transitively to disciple, that is, enroll as scholar: - be disciple, instruct, teach.

Teaching (G1321) (to learn); to teach (in the same broad application): - teach.

Why the change from "preach" to "teach"? As stated a moment ago, there is a lot more detail here. I will give you some of it to make this point clear. The reason He only instructs to "teach" here is because of the timing of Matthew, which is that He has returned feet down on the Mount of Olives. This is the reason I added verse 18 there for you as well, which tells us that now all power has been given to Him in heaven and on earth, as we read happens at the 7th trumpet.

> ***Revelation 11:15*** *(KJV)*
> **15** And the seventh angel sounded; and there were great voices in heaven, saying, **The kingdoms of this world are become the kingdoms of our Lord**, and of his Christ and he shall reign for ever and ever.

But there is more. Let's read verse 20 more closely. He tells them to teach the world the things they are to "observe" about Him. And then goes on to tell them, "and I am with you always, even until the end of the world!" Why? Because He has returned.

As we now know, at the 7th Trumpet, Jesus will have returned and there will be no more need for preaching, because the WHOLE WORLD will have seen His coming when all power in heaven and earth will now be His. And He will be here reigning for the 1000 years until, "the end of the world".

None of this is spoken about in Luke or Mark. In fact, in both of their gospels, He is either "carried up" or "received up" into heaven. Let me briefly show you that next.

"CARRIED UP / RECEIVED UP / RETURNED AND STAYING"

We see here in these last chapters, Jesus is being taken to heaven or at least He is being taken to heaven in two of the three gospels.

CARRIED UP

> ***Luke 24:51*** *(KJV)*
> **51** And it came to pass, while he blessed them, he was parted from them, and **carried up (G399)** into heaven.

Carried up (G399) which means bear, bring (carry, lead) up.

And like a bride, they are **"carried" up,** over the threshold. Escape!

RECEIVED UP

Mark 16:19 *(KJV)*
19 So then after the Lord had spoken unto them, he was **received up (G353)** into heaven, and sat on the right hand of God.

Received up (G353) which means to take up: - receive up, take (in, unto, up).

And like guests who are invited to a wedding, they are **"received" up,** to the banquet. Rapture!

RETURNED and STAYING

Matthew 28:20 *(KJV)*
20 Teaching them to observe all things whatsoever I have commanded you: and, lo, **I am with you alway**, **even unto the end of the world**. Amen.

Jesus is here representing the people group of both Luke and Mark, who will both be taken to heaven in their portions on time. Pre-tribulation before Seals, LUKE, and Mid-tribulation end of Seals, MARK. Whereas in MATTHEW, there is none of this conversation and so He is not representing a people group. It is simply Him returning feet down on the Mount of Olives at the **end**.

I am not done yet. I want to be sure you are understanding how to "see and read" His revelation of the End Times hidden within His word, for such a time as this.

THE ABOMINATION OF DESOLATION
(SPOKEN OF BY DANIEL THE PROPHET)

The abomination of desolation spoken of in the Olivet discourse of Matthew 24, is a very famous scripture and prophecy. But like many other parts has been misunderstood considering its timing. You are going to see why we also find this conversation in Mark, and why it is never spoken about. As well as why Luke does not mention it at all. As a refresher, I want to remind you that the first shall be last and the last shall be first. In the End Times it will be Luke, Mark, Matthew. So let's have a look at where we find it and where we do not.

In Luke's discourse we read nothing of it, but instead it tells us in the same section -

> ***Luke 21:20*** *(KJV)*
> **20** And when ye shall see Jerusalem compassed with armies, then know that **the desolation thereof is nigh**.

Jesus tells them here about seeing Jerusalem surrounded and to know that when they see this, Jerusalem is "about" to be attacked and destroyed.

Desolation (G2050) From G2049; despoliation: - desolation. (G2049) **to lay waste** (literally or figuratively): - (bring to, make) desolate (-ion), come to nought.

In other words, completely destroyed. But when is He telling them this? That was part of the mystery. The revelation is that it is during the "Son of Man's 40 days warning", as we will read in the following section about, called "The Sign of Jonah".

So why is the abomination not found here? Because Luke's discussion is about a short period of time right before the Tribulation years literally begin, called the 40 days of the Son of Man. After which they will have not heeded the warning and Jerusalem will be attacked. And this will now begin the Tribulation.

> ***Mark 13:14*** *(KJV)*
> But when ye shall see **the abomination of desolation**, spoken of **by Daniel** the prophet, ***standing where it ought not***, (let him that readeth understand,)

You will see "where it ought not" is very different from what Matthew says. And here again the churches have simply ignored this difference in Mark. But there is another incredible revelation hidden in it.

The word "standing" also means "place", which would read to "place where it ought not", and during the time of Seals it is about the sleeping church, which is still a reference to the Body, that we know as the Temple of Christ. Making this the abomination being spoken of in Mark, the reference to the "mark of the beast" spoken about in -

> ***Revelation 13:16-17*** *(KJV)*
> **16** And he causeth all, both small and great, rich and poor, free and bond, **to receive a mark in their right hand, or in their foreheads**:
> **17** And that no man might buy or sell, **save he**

that had the mark, or the name of the beast, or the number of his name.

This "mark of the beast" is to be avoided at all cost, even unto death if necessary. And just as this mark will be "around" the time of the middle of Seals, so will the Mark group still be here who were left behind. And right around this time, I would say a little earlier, is when the antichrist figure, who so many have heard about, will be given greater power to continue for 42 months as we read in Revelation 13:5.

But how is it that we are told it is "spoken of by Daniel". Yet both Mark and Matthew then have a reference? The answer is that Daniel speaks about it TWICE! It was simply never understood. Here is the one that speaks to Mark's reference.

Daniel 11:31-32 *(KJV)*
31 And arms shall stand on his part, and they shall pollute the sanctuary of strength, and shall take away the daily sacrifice, and they shall place the **abomination that maketh desolate**.
32 And such as do wickedly against the covenant *shall* ***he*** *corrupt* by flatteries: but the people that do know their God shall be strong, and do exploits.

You will note that as you read this chapter in Daniel that there is all building up to this "he" coming who will corrupt people with flatteries and will then go on to "speak" terrible things against GOD.

Daniel 11:36 *(KJV)*
And the king shall do according to his will; and he

shall exalt himself, and magnify himself above every **god**, and shall speak marvelous things against **the God of gods.**

This is the antichrist when he comes into that great power. But it is very important to note that he **does not claim to be GOD**. He only magnifies himself above the "little g" or lower case "g" gods. And he only speaks blasphemous words against GOD. Again never claiming he is the upper case "G" GOD. We read this also in Revelation 13 about him. And this is because his abomination of desolation against mankind, is this coming "mark of the beast" everyone will be required to have in order to get food or work, as well as to have everyone worship him.

But now this brings us to Matthew's version and why, as you will see, he says "stand in the holy place".

> ***Matthew 24:15*** *(KJV)*
> When ye therefore shall see **the abomination of desolation**, spoken of **by Daniel** the prophet, **stand in the holy place**, whoso readeth, let him understand.

It certainly may sound similar, but you are about to understand it is undoubtedly not the same.

Let us not forget that we are reading from Matthew's gospel, and that the time of the sleeping church has ended and the rapture has already happened. We are now in the time of Trumpets and remember who had come down on Mount Zion at the end of Seals? In an upcoming chapter called *"The Revelation of Daniel 9"*, you will come to understand that there will be a point when the Lord on Mount Zion will leave, because satan will have finally lost his battle in heaven against Michael, as we read in -

Revelation 12:7-9 *(KJV)*
7 And there was war in heaven: Michael and his
angels fought against the dragon; and the dragon
fought and his angels,
8 And prevailed not; neither was their place found
any more in heaven.
9 And the great dragon was cast out, that old
serpent, called the Devil, and Satan, which
deceiveth the whole world: he **was cast out into
the earth**, and his angels were cast out with him.

This period of time is about mid-Trumpets time. The confusion taught on all of this is also rooted in the fact that it has been taught to us that the antichrist is satan, when in fact he is not. However, they work together hand in hand and the antichrist gets his power from him. However, if they were one, why does Revelation tell us about all three, including the false prophet who will be working with the antichrist during Seals? Have each of them spirits like until frogs come out of them"? I will go into more detail into this in the chapter called *"Revealing Revelation"*.

Revelation 16:13 *(KJV)*
13 And I saw three unclean spirits like frogs come
out of the mouth **of the dragon**, and out of the
mouth **of the beast**, and out of the mouth **of the
false prophet**.

This brings us back to how Matthew can have another version and this one being the one that will "stand in the holy place". You will also understand in the chapter about Daniel 9, that during the first half of Trumpets, the city, streets and temple will get rebuilt in Jerusalem only after the land has rested during the time of Seals. Making this Matthew portion, which is to the Jews, the point at which the temple will have been built and satan being cast down at the time frame of the 5th trumpet. At which time he will "stand in the holy place", the actual temple that had been rebuilt. Causing the second abomination of desolation spoken of by Daniel in chapter 12.

> ***Daniel 12:11*** *(KJV)*
> **11** And from the time that the daily sacrifice shall be taken away, and **the abomination that maketh desolate** set up, there shall be a thousand two hundred and ninety days.

Which now also confirms to us what it says in -

> ***2 Thessalonians 2:4*** *(KJV)*
> **4** Who opposeth and exalteth himself above all that is called God, or that is worshipped; so that **he as God sitteth in the temple of God, shewing himself that he is God**.

These are not the same words or actions as the antichrist's, nor will the antichrist have a physical third temple to step into during the Seals. Clearly once more revealing to us two separate periods of time, Seals and Trumpets, for two different groups of people.

THE SIGN OF JONAH IS NOT THE SAME IN EACH GOSPEL

This is another one of those revelations where there is much more to this teaching than what we will discuss here, especially the first portion of 40 days. One of the many great revelations that has been revealed through the differences in the three synoptic gospels, is the 40 days warning of the Son of Man. There will be a chapter dedicated to this topic specifically called "*The 40 days of the Son of Man"*. This portion is to highlight the differences in the three gospels of when Jesus spoke regarding "as Jonah was". All of the stories you have read thus far are clearly revealing the purpose of these differences in the gospels. It was all done with an insight of giving us the, "what is to come". And not only is this one also going to prove that, more than that it will bring greater clarity as to what Jesus did OR did not yet do. It will also clear up what many people have pointed to as, "a clear contradiction" in the gospels. One of which is that out of the three gospels mentioning the sign of Jonah, in Mark, Jesus says no sign will be given and leaves. I am not really sure how anyone had explained it before without the revelation of any real End Time understanding. Just like so many other parts of scripture that had us scratching our heads for generations.

THE 40 DAYS WARNING (in Luke)

> ***Luke 11:29-30*** *(KJV)*
> **29** ... and there shall no sign be given it, but the sign of Jonas the prophet.

30 For as **Jonas was a sign** unto the Ninevites **so shall also the Son of man be** to this generation.

For context about what is spoken here, Jonah was sent by GOD to a place called Nineveh to give them a warning that destruction was coming in 40 days should they not repent. Jesus tells them that as Jonah did, so shall also the Son of Man do, which is another name for Jesus. Not that He would be going to the same place, but that He, the Son of Man, would also at some point, give a 40 day warning as Jonah did.

Now many, if not all, have been taught that Jesus fulfilled this particular scripture already after His resurrection when He remained for 40 days. But, He did not. We do not have a single conversation of Him, during His 40 days on earth after His resurrection, giving any warning to any nation(s) to come to repentance or be destroyed after 40 days. Here is what we are told in Acts 1.

Acts 1:2-4 *(KJV)*

2 Until the day in which he was taken up, after that he through the Holy Ghost had given commandments unto the apostles whom he had chosen:

3 To whom also he shewed himself alive after his passion by many infallible proofs, being **seen of them forty days**, and speaking of the things pertaining to the kingdom of God:

4 And, being assembled together with them, commanded them that they should not depart from Jerusalem, but wait for the promise of the Father, which, saith he, ye have heard of me.

There is not a single warning to them or anyone to repent or suffer destruction after His 40 days. For years we have been told that this scripture was only about His 40 days after His resurrection and nothing more. But how are we to understand the wording that He would do as Jonah did? We have also been told that it was represented as 40 years. And you will see in some of the other teachings in this book that days in scripture can most certainly have a clear representation as years. However, we still have an issue with this, because we can and have proven that Jesus truly did get crucified and resurrected at Passover of 33AD. So if you use the days as years count for the warning, how does 33AD + 40 years equal when Jerusalem was destroyed in 70AD? It does not. The answer to this mystery is that it has NOT YET been fulfilled. Each account of this story in the gospels is prophecy… "is to come"!

NO SIGN (in Mark)

> ***Mark 8:12-13*** *(KJV)*
> **12** And he sighed deeply in his spirit, and saith,
> Why doth this generation seek after a sign? verily I
> say unto you, There shall **no sign** be given unto this
> generation.
> **13** And he left them, and entering into the ship
> again departed to the other side.

Looking at this, we can understand why there would be apparent valid comments defining this as a contradiction. The incredible answer to this is found in each of the three gospels right before the story of the

Mount of Transfiguration. I will touch on it here just briefly to make the point.

> ***Mark 9:1*** *(KJV)*
> And he said unto them, Verily I say unto you, That there be some of them that stand here, which shall not taste of death, till **they have seen** the kingdom of God come with power.

This scripture is also found in Luke and Matthew, and also right before the Transfiguration story, but each once again, varies in the language. My focus here is on Mark. The other gospels will be discussed in another chapter called, "*The Differences and the Truth*". In Mark's version the language is past tense, "have seen". Meaning they will "have seen" the kingdom of GOD come, but will not be going to it right away at the seeing of it coming. Now remember, we are in Mark's gospel and we have been explaining that Mark is the left behind church that would go through Seals before the mid-tribulation rapture, after Seal judgments.

So let's go have a look at the Seal judgments in the book of Revelation. Starting with the last seal, the 6th seal.

> ***Revelation 6:16-17*** *(KJV)*
> **16** And said to the mountains and rocks, Fall on us, and **hide us from the face of him that sitteth on the throne**, and from the wrath of the Lamb:
> **17** For the great day of his wrath is come; and who shall be able to stand?

Telling us that people everywhere will see His coming and will be terrified, but not raptured right away. Now as an important side note, do not confuse this coming with His feet down on the Mount of Olives. You will understand this a little further on into the book, but for a heads up, this is Him coming in the clouds on Mount Zion. Then in chapter 7 of Revelation we see a group called the 144,000 who are being sealed first before anything else happens. AFTER this the Mark group, who we know as the rapture group, called the "great multitude", before the Lord.

> ***Revelation 7:9-10*** *(KJV)*
> **9** After this I beheld, and, lo, ***a great multitude, which no man could number, of all nations, and kindreds, and people, and tongues, stood before the throne, and before the Lamb***, clothed with white robes, and palms in their hands;
> **10** And cried with a loud voice, saying, Salvation to our God which sitteth upon the throne, and unto the Lamb.

It is clear that the Mark group of the great multitude, at mid-tribulation after the Seal judgments, are now raptured standing before the throne, **AFTER they "have seen"** Him coming with power. Bringing home the point that the Mark people group will not be given any sign.

I said I would also touch on the Mount of Transfiguration story here as well to make the point for Mark's time. It is going to have you saying, wait what are you saying about the years? But fear not, you will fully understand this question in the next chapter, "*When The Years Just Don't Add Up*".

We see in Mark's Transfiguration story the following -

> ***Mark 9:2*** *(KJV)*
> **2** And **after six days** Jesus taketh with him Peter, and James, and John, and leadeth them up into an high mountain apart by themselves: and he was transfigured before them.

And a few verses later we see Jesus finally coming down "the mountain", think Mount Zion we just spoke about, after the events that took place on it. And look who is right there -

> ***Mark 9:14-15*** *(KJV)*
> **14** And when he came to his disciples, he saw a **great multitude** about them, and the scribes questioning with them.
> **15** And straightway all the people, when they beheld him, were greatly amazed, *and running to him saluted him.*

The same type and shadow story of having been on a mountain with a group of people first, then a great multitude gathering to Him in great joy. But there was something more to this. Did you notice how it said AFTER 6 days? If you recall, "days" can also represent in prophecy "years". Now you might think 6 seals, 6 days? However, what is really being given to us here, as well as in the other two gospels, in the same story is a major clue to the revelation of the true time frame of the whole tribulation. This will be revealed in greater detail as mentioned in the next chapter, *"When The Years Just Don't Add up"*. But the clue here is 6 days are prophetic as years. Meaning, After 6 years, of the six judgments of Seals, they will then see the Lord coming on heavenly

Mount Zion in the clouds. And the great multitude will be raptured into the 7th year or the sabbath year, before the Trumpet judgments begin. Wow! I know that is a lot to take in, but it will become increasingly clear shortly.

3 DAYS AND 3 NIGHTS (in Matthew)

> ***Matthew 12:40*** *(KJV)*
> For as Jonas was **three days** **<u>and</u>** **three nights** in the whale's belly <u>**so shall the Son of man be *three days and three nights*** in the heart of the earth</u>.

We can see here again in Matthew's version that it is different. And this is one we have also been taught in the churches that it was fulfilled by Jesus at His death and resurrection. But you will see and understand for yourselves that <u>it was not</u>. It was prophetic and <u>not yet fulfilled</u>.

I am sure for many of you all of this is causing a bit of an overload. There is so much that has already been revealed that needs time to be processed. I understand. As you take the time to seek these things for yourselves and pray for the Holy Spirit to guide you and reveal them to you, He will.

Now let me show you how scripture shows <u>it was not possible</u> that Jesus had fulfilled this.

> ***Luke 9:22*** *(KJV)*
> **22** Saying, The Son of man must suffer many things, and be rejected of the elders and chief priests and scribes, and be slain, <u>and be raised **the third day**</u>.

This conversation took place while these two men were walking with Jesus and didn't realize it was Him having resurrected.

Luke 24:20-21 *(KJV)*
20 And how the chief priests and our rulers delivered him to be condemned to death, and have crucified him.
21 But we trusted that it had been he which should have redeemed Israel: <u>and beside all this</u>, **today <u>is the third day</u>** since these things were done.

Luke 24:46 *(KJV)*
46 And said unto them, *Thus it is written*, and thus it behoved <u>Christ to suffer, and to rise from the dead</u> **<u>the third day</u>**:

Matthew 17:22-23 *(KJV)*
22 And while they abode in Galilee, Jesus said unto them, The Son of man shall be betrayed into the hands of men:
23 And they shall kill him, <u>and **the third day** *he shall be raised again*</u>. And they were exceedingly sorry.

Matthew 20:19 *(KJV)*
19 And shall deliver him to the Gentiles to mock, and to scourge, and to crucify him: <u>and **the third day** *he shall rise again*</u>.

Are you seeing the wording? <u>Not once are we being told He would be resurrected **AFTER** 3 day**S** and 3 night**S**</u>!

EVERY single occasion tells us <u>He resurrected **on the third day**</u>. However, after 3 days and 3 nights would mean day 4! This has caused such a tremendous amount of confusion in the church for those who have questioned and tried to understand how could He have then resurrected in 33AD on the Sunday? Of course this is another revelation in itself. But I will give you the quick answer. When you study the wording of His death and resurrection you will find out He said it **began from;** when He would be taken into the hands of sinful men, then crucified, then resurrected, and that those three events together consist of His resurrection on the third day! Which for those of you still wondering, the third day means about two and a half days. He resurrected on the third day early in the morning, which means during the early daylight of the third day. Hence, the "Jonah Prophecy" has still to be fulfilled sometime at the end of tribulation.

The church has been teaching all their understanding from the perspective of Matthew, and as you have come to see, Matthew is not for the bride or church, but for the Jews. I am not coming against all pastors and teachers who have taught this. I am simply making the point that their perspective on having taught it this way has been similar to what the chief priests and Pharisees taught. That is something no pastor or teacher ever wants to be a part of.

Matthew 27:62-63 *(KJV)*
62 Now the next day, that followed the day of the preparation, the chief priests and Pharisees came together unto Pilate,
63 Saying, Sir, we remember that that deceiver

said, while he was yet alive, **After three days** I will rise again.

He did not say **after** three days, He said **the third day**! And that one time where He said the Son of Man would be as Jonah was, that He would be three days and three nights in the heart of the earth, was prophetic. Just as He said about the 40 days of the Son of Man - prophecy for the End Times!

PREPARING THE PASSOVER

This revelation is more focused on what is being said in Luke and Mark than in Matthew. But you are also going to see another revelation built into this that will become fully revealed to you when you get to the chapter called, "*The Books have Opened!*" If you thought all this was amazing, wait until you get to that chapter. I am boasting in the Lord's faithfulness! You will understand why we called it "*The Books have Opened!*". But let's not get too ahead of ourselves (I mean me. I get a little excited about teaching on all these things, sometimes bouncing from one place to another). Let's start with Luke.

Luke 22:10-12 *(KJV)*
10 And he said unto them, Behold, when ye are entered into the city, there shall a man meet you, bearing a pitcher of water; follow him into the house where he entereth in.
11 And ye shall say unto the goodman of the house, The Master saith unto thee, Where is the guestchamber, where I shall eat the passover with my disciples?

12 And <u>he shall shew you **a large upper room (G508) furnished**: there make ready</u>.

Mark 14:13-15 *(KJV)*
13 And he sendeth forth two of his disciples, and saith unto them, Go ye into the city, and there shall meet you a man bearing a pitcher of water: follow him.
14 And wheresoever he shall go in, say ye to the goodman of the house, The Master saith, Where is the guestchamber, where I shall eat the passover with my disciples?
15 And <u>he will shew you **a large upper room(G508) furnished *and prepared (G2092)***: there make ready for us</u>.

Room (G508) means; <u>***above the ground***</u>, that is, (properly) the second floor of a building; <u>used for a dome</u> or a balcony on the upper story: - <u>upper room</u>. Total KJV occurrences: **2**

What is even more telling of this word "room" that is being used here, is that it is <u>only used twice</u> in the Bible. And just as we read a little earlier about the groups of people being represented in Luke and Mark being taken to heaven, this "upper room" being discussed is yet another type and shadow of both these groups going to the large upper room for them in heaven.

You will also notice there is an extra word added to Mark's version, "<u>prepared</u>".

Prepared (G2092) that is, ready: - prepared, (made) ready (-iness, to our hand)

Now at first, this word simply seems obvious and would otherwise hold no other value than what it says. But knowing what you have begun to understand you may now say, yes that is strange? Why there in Mark and not in Luke? Questions like this are what bring about revelation to those that seek them out.

I began this topic by also telling you there was more to this revelation based on what I called the "*The Books have Opened!*" and part of that applies to this word "prepared". Now without getting detailed here, I am going to share with you an incredible revelation that is found in the gospel of John. I know our focus is the synoptic gospels, and it still is, however I wanted to show you this to make a point here as to why Mark has this word. But in doing so, if I only share "where" it is in John, you will not have the context of "why" it is there, in that specific chapter of John.

And that is that the gospel of John has built into it what I call, "the chapters to years". You will understand more as you come to that chapter in the book. As you know John has 21 chapters. So a chapter to year would mean 21 years. And the way to begin to wrap your mind around it, is to think of the story of Jacob and the years of work he did for Leah and Rachel and then the cattle. John's hidden End Time revelation is based on those working of years. So would make the first 7 chapters/years of John the type and shadow of the first 7 years Jacob worked for his first bride. We know he expected Rachel after the first 7 years, but ended up getting Leah, which is also an End Time story unto itself. It tells us in Genesis 29 that those first 7 years "flew by because he loved her so". So now if you look at what happens after the first 7 chapters of John, chapter 8 begins with a woman caught in adultery. Jesus is bent over as the crowd asks Him what He thinks they should do with her. And as many know, the story goes on to say, Jesus said, "He who is without sin let him cast the first stone." And they left convicted within themselves knowing they had all sinned. Then Jesus bends over again to write in the sand. And when He looked up again, all those that had been accusing her were now gone. And it then says;

> ***John 8:9-10*** *(KJV)*
> **9** And they, which heard it, being convicted by
> their own conscience, went out one by one,
> beginning at the eldest, even unto the last: and
> **Jesus was left alone, and the woman standing in the midst.**
> **10** When Jesus had lifted up himself, and saw none
> but the woman,...

Who does this Gentile woman caught in adultery represent? And Jesus having been bent down on the ground, looks up and sees no other but her standing before Him. What does this sound like to you? Kind of like a wedding proposal? Bent down on one knee, looking up and only seeing her.

You are probably asking yourself, "What does this have to do with Mark's version having the word "prepared"?" You would be right in asking that question, because it has nothing to do with it. It was Luke's Gentile Bride representation that comes first. And I felt I needed to lay a little groundwork for you and like I said earlier, not just say here is John 14 for Mark and this is what it means. It will also help you with a little understanding so that once you get to the chapter about all this in greater detail you will already have a head start.

So now after Jacob has finished his first 7 years and gets Leah as his first bride, he is told for Rachel, the one he really wanted, that he could have her too, but that he would need to complete another 7 years. So if we follow along in John now to chapter 14, we find;

> ***John 14:1-3*** *(KJV)*
> **1** Let not your heart be troubled: ye believe in God, believe also in me.
> **2** In my Father's house are many mansions: if it were not so, I would have told you. <u>I go to **prepare (G2090)** a place for you</u>.
> **3** <u>And if I go and **prepare (G2090)** a place for you</u>, ***I will <u>come again</u>***, and *receive you unto myself; that where I am, there ye may be also.*

Prepare (G2090) **From <u>G2092</u>**; to prepare: - <u>prepare, provide, make ready</u>. It comes from the root word G2092 the word "prepared" from Mark's version. It's simply that the tense of the word of one is letting them know He is going to "prepare" it.

It just so happens it was in that chapter of John where He was speaking to a group of people letting them know He would "<u>come again</u>" for them <u>with</u> this place "<u>prepared</u>".

Since we have come this far in the Jacob to John, years to chapters, and have shown Luke and Mark's time represented in the type and shadow of Pre-trib, Escape of the Bride, and Rapture of the Left Behind church, why not bring it to the end with Matthew's representation?

> ***Matthew 26:17-19*** *(KJV)*
> **17** Now the first day of the feast of unleavened bread the disciples came to Jesus, saying unto him, Where wilt thou that we prepare for thee to eat the passover?
> **18** And he said, Go into the city to such a man, and say unto him, The Master saith, My time is at hand; I will keep the passover at thy house with my disciples.
> **19** And the disciples did as Jesus had appointed them; and they made ready the passover.

The conversation here is not the same as Luke or Mark's version. Not the same description of the man, nor any mention of an "upper room" neither "furnished" nor "prepared". Well if you recall only Luke and Mark's groups go to heaven. Matthew's group remains on earth, for the Kingdom of Heaven on earth at the return of Christ "feet down" for the following 1000 year reign. Not as the other two who are in the Kingdom of GOD, what we call "the" heaven. So that covers why there is no mention of any "upper room" here. But for the "timing" of Matthew's version let's continue in Jacob's story to John's chapter to years.

Next in Jacob's story we read he then works 6 more years for the cattle. And at the end of those years we read in Genesis 31 that he has completed working for his father in law a total of 20 years (7 easy ones received Leah

"Luke", 7 more for Rachel "Mark" and final 6 for cattle "Matthew"). And so if we now go to John chapter 20 we find it is the resurrection of Jesus and His final instructions to His disciples.

> ***John 20:19-21*** *(KJV)*
> **19** Then the same day at evening, being the first
> day of the week, **when the doors were shut** where
> the disciples were assembled for fear of the Jews,
> **came Jesus and stood in the midst**, and saith
> unto them, Peace be unto you.
> **20** And when he had so said, he shewed unto them
> his hands and his side. Then were the disciples glad,
> when they saw the Lord.
> **21** Then said Jesus to them again, Peace be unto
> you: as my Father hath sent me, even so send I you.

The literal type and shadow of His return feet down at the end of the 6 years of Trumpets.

And did you notice? In all the synoptic gospels the story of Jesus' return at the resurrection is found in the last chapter of their books, with the final instructions Jesus gives them. However, in John it is in the second last chapter of his book.

It is the end of the story. Even though there is "one" chapter left in John (more on why in the coming chapters), this is all a representation of Him having returned after 20 years.

Now what should be on your minds at this point is, what on earth is he talking about after 20 years? Or why 7 easy years to Luke's group, leaving 13 more years, of which 7 are for Mark's group and the last 6 for Matthew's group? And why does John then still have "one" more chapter/year?

These are all great questions and they will all be answered in what awaits you in the next great revelation that began to be received after "Who The Gospels Are Speaking To". That is why I saved this Jacob to John story last. Leading you into those questions and take you into chapter two. Chapter two along with this first one are what I have termed, "***The 2 Keys of End Time Understanding***". I pray this has begun to bless you and that the following chapter will bring even greater levels of End Time understanding and clarity to you.

GOD'S HARVEST MODEL

I would like to just quickly draw your attention to the harvest model found in scripture that is applicable to LUKE, MARK, and MATTHEW and the 14 year tribulation timeline. We read about this harvest model in Leviticus 23 and 19.

> ***Leviticus 23: 22*** *(KJV)*
> **22** And when ye reap the harvest of your land, thou shalt not make clean riddance of the corners of thy field when thou reapest, neither shalt thou gather any gleaning of thy harvest: thou shalt leave them unto the poor, and to the stranger: I am the Lord your God.
>
> ***Leviticus 19: 9 - 10*** *(KJV)*
> **9** And when ye reap the harvest of your land, thou shalt not wholly reap the corners of thy field,

neither shalt thou gather the gleanings of thy harvest.
10 And thou shalt not glean thy vineyard, neither shalt thou gather [every] grape of thy vineyard; thou shalt leave them for the poor and stranger: I [am] the LORD your God.

There are 3 specific harvest models in scripture:

1. The Barley Harvest
2. The Wheat Harvest
3. The Grape Harvest

And the harvest model of each consists of 3 parts:

1. The first fruits
2. The main harvest
3. The corners or gleanings

The **Barley Harvest** is the harvest that Jesus represented, as the first fruits, brought in, of which the main harvest were the believers during Christ's period, and those spoken of in Matthew 27:52-53 who were raised from the dead. The corners (gleanings) are those few remaining who come to believe at the very end of this cycle.

The **Wheat Harvest** is also divided into a first fruits, which is the Bride of Christ, that will have escaped all these things coming, the main harvest is the left behind or great multitude that we read of standing before the Lamb in Revelation 7: 9 - 11 that have gone through the Seals judgment, having been raptured, and the corners (gleanings) are again those few remaining who come in at the very end of this harvest cycle.

We then have the **Grape Harvest**, which is that of the Jews/Judah, of which the <u>first fruits</u> are the 144,000 as we read in Revelation 14: 1, the <u>main harvest</u> is the Jews/Judah that will return unto their Messiah at His coming feet down, having gone through Trumpets, and the <u>corners (gleanings)</u> are again those few towards the very end of the cycle when the Lord 7th year comes to an end.

**For an easy reference, please see the two Harvest Models in the Appendix.*

I want to close out this chapter with an encouraging parable Jesus gives us in Luke that I really enjoy reading and sharing.

> ***Luke 18:1-8*** *(KJV)*
> **1** And he spake a parable unto them to this end, that men ought always to pray, and not to faint;
> **2** Saying, There was in a city a judge, which feared not God, neither regarded man:
> **3** And there was a widow in that city; and she came unto him, saying, Avenge me of mine adversary.
> **4** And he would not for a while: but afterward he said within himself, Though I fear not God, nor regard man;
> **5** Yet because this widow troubleth me, I will avenge her, lest by her continual coming she

weary me.
6 And the Lord said, Hear what the unjust
judge saith.
7 And shall not God avenge his own elect,
which cry day and night unto him, though he
bears long with them?
8 I tell you that he will avenge them speedily.
Nevertheless when the Son of man cometh,
shall he find faith on the earth?

CHAPTER 2

WHEN THE YEARS JUST DON'T ADD UP

Have you ever thought to yourself that you just cannot see how everything we have been told could fit into 7 years? Many have been struggling with this thought.

In this chapter we would like to present some examples in scripture and some research, of which there are plenty more, that clearly confirms that the Tribulation will actually be 2 sets of 7 years for a total of 14 years, and not the 7 years we have been taught. I will also be showing you the Strong's Concordance meaning that comes with each word we will be discussing. Every word in Scripture is assigned a number which either has an H (Hebrew) or G (Greek) meaning for our clarification and understanding. This has been a great source of help in having been able to open the End Time understanding. For example H7103 or G7103.

FOURTEEN YEARS SPOKEN OF BY PAUL

I had just recently started to understand who the gospels were speaking to, when I came across this scripture written by Paul. I realized I had never heard anyone give any explanation for it in any End Time teaching. And as you are about to understand, there is a good reason for that. How could these verses ever be explained in only a 7 year understanding?

2 Corinthians 12:2 - 4; and 14 *(KJV)*
2 I knew a man in Christ <u>**above fourteen years**</u>

ago, (whether in the body, I cannot tell; or whether out of the body, I cannot tell: God knoweth;) ***such an one*** **caught up** to the **third heaven**.
3 And I knew such a man, (whether in the body, or out of the body, I cannot tell: God knoweth;)
4 How that he ***was*** **caught up** into **paradise**, and heard unspeakable words, which it is not lawful for a man to utter.

And when we get down to verse 14, we find out he is speaking in this chapter as now coming the third time.

14 Behold, the **third time** I am ready ***to come to you***, and I will not be burdensome to you: for I seek not yours but you: for the children ought not to lay up for the parents, but the parents for the children.

THE FIRST GROUP - LUKE / BRIDE

You will note in verse 2 that it says "**such an one**" which is the word (G5108). As well as the words "**caught up"** which is (G726), to the **third heaven.**

G5108 means "of this sort or like", meaning this first event is **"like"** a "caught up". G726 means **harpazō** (har-pad'-zo) from a derivative of G138; to seize (in various applications): - **catch (away, up), pluck, pull, take (by force)**. Or as most have come to understand it, Rapture!

So verse 2 reads as: Above 14 years ago, one was "like" a "rapture" taken to the Third Heaven.

When we refer to the Bride of Christ being raptured, we in this ministry, use the word "Escape" which comes from Luke 21: 36.

Luke 21:36 *(KJV)*

Watch ye therefore, and pray always that ye may be accounted worthy to **escape ALL** these things that shall come to pass, and to stand before the Son of man.

This "escape" from all things that shall come to pass, i*s the "like" a "rapture" to the Third Heaven* where they will be standing before the Son of Man.

That was only verse 2 speaking of the first event. But as we continue reading through verse 3 and 4, we see Paul then telling us of another event.

THE SECOND GROUP - MARK / LEFT BEHIND

In verses 3 - 4 of 2 Corinthians 12 you will note the words: And I knew such a man... How that he "**was" caught up (G726)** into **paradise**.

This second group is not defined as the first, being "like", but is clearly telling us this one, **"was"** "caught up", G726 **harpazō** (har-pad'-zo) from a derivative of G138; to seize (in various applications): - **catch (away, up), pluck, pull, take (by force)**.

Again, as most have come to understand it, raptured! However, this time not to the third heaven as per verse 2, but to paradise.

Now that is pretty clear. It tells us that **the first one was LIKE a rapture/ harpazō** and **the second one WAS a rapture/ harpazō!**

We find greater clarity of this exact wording, "was caught up", in Revelation 12: 5, which also helps us understand this timing.

> ***Revelation 12:5*** *(KJV)*
> And she brought forth a man child, who was to rule all nations with a rod of iron: and her child **was caught up (G726)** unto God, and to his throne.

I am certain many of you have heard that this verse is speaking to what is known as the Pre-tribulation rapture of the church. However, this clearly must be questioned now. Because according to the understanding by Paul, this ***"was"*** *"caught up"*, is not the first rapture-like event. It is the second! And we can prove this out more. Let's go to:

> ***Isaiah 66:7*** *(KJV)*
> **7** ***Before*** *she travailed* (H2342), *she brought forth*, **before** *her pain came*, *she was delivered* of a man child.

Many have used this verse to prove that the Pre-tribulation will happen first. The key here is, "**Before** she travails", which is H2342 and means; to writhe in pain, travail (with pain), be in pain, - bear, (make to) bring forth. I think you get the picture.

So this is telling us "**before**" she begins travailing in pain she brings forth. There was a birth. This **"before"** truly is the Pre-tribulation rapture or as we call it "escape". And this escape will be that of the bride of Christ. However, we have an issue here with what the churches have taught. Because if the "**was**" caught up we read about in

Rev.12:5 is to be the Pre-tribulation rapture, why is it happening **AFTER** the travailing in birth pains and the birth following those travailing pains from verses 2 - 5? The answer is that this "**was**" caught up in Revelation 12: 5, is not Isaiah 66:7's Pre-tribulation rapture. It is Paul's second event called, "**was**" caught up" of 2 Corinthians 12: 3 - 4. And Paul's first event "**like**" caught up, is Isaiah 66:7's "**before**" **she travailed**, Pre-tribulation escape/rapture! This explains why the one goes to the third heaven and the other to paradise.

In other words:

ESCAPE - 2 Corinthians 12: 2 goes with Isaiah 66: 7

RAPTURE - 2 Corinthians 12: 3 - 4 goes with Revelation 12:5

But Paul is not done yet. Remember in verse 14 he goes on to tell us, "the third time"? We have just covered the Pre-tribulation escape to Luke, which is **above 14 years**. We have also covered the second event as the Mid-tribulation rapture of Mark, which will be **the 7th year rest of Seals**. Who is left? The third and final group of course, is Matthew. And this is the group in the End Time type and shadow, that this whole conversation is being spoken to. He is recounting to them the events that have happened prior to **his coming** the **third** time.

THE THIRD GROUP - MATTHEW / JEWS

> ***2 Corinthians 12: 14*** *(KJV)*
> **14** Behold, the **third time** I am ready **to come to you**; and I will not be burdensome to you: for I seek

not yours but you: for the children ought not to lay up for the parents, but the parents for the children.

Paul, in this chapter, is the type of Christ. And we saw that the first and second time it was a taking away to another place. Yet this **third time** he says he is **coming to them**. And what do we know this means at the end? The Lord is returning feet down on the Mount of Olives. And the promised Millennial Reign will soon begin with each Tribe finally receiving their land inheritance.

The order of events will be:

1. *The first group* **ESCAPE** (Luke/The Bride), **above (before)** the fourteen years begin.
2. Followed by *the second group* that will be the **RAPTURE** (Mark/Left Behind) in the 7th year of rest toward the end of seals.
3. Finally *the third group* that will see Him **COMING DOWN TO THEM** (Matthew/Jews) at the end of 13 years, to fulfill the 14th and final year.

ON THE MOUNT OF TRANSFIGURATION

I am purposely discussing the Mount of Transfiguration first before the story of Jacob. It is a great place for us to begin in order for you to see the bigger picture of the "year counts". Of which the first portion of years are nearing their end, as I write this. This first portion is what you have heard me call, the **escape** of the Bride of Christ, which will be one of the greatest events in all of human history.

However, in this section I am only going to share the revelation of the Mount of Transfiguration regarding the

End Time years count. The greater revelation of the rest of this Transfiguration story is found in the chapter *"The Differences and The Truth"*.

> ***Luke 9:28*** *(KJV)*
> And it came to pass **about an eight days** after these sayings, he took Peter and John and James, and went up into a mountain to pray.
>
> ***Mark 9:2*** *(KJV)*
> And **after six days** Jesus taketh with him Peter, and James, and John, and leadeth them up into an high mountain apart by themselves: and he was transfigured before them.
>
> ***Matthew 17:1*** *(KJV)*
> And **after six days** Jesus taketh Peter, James, and John his brother, and bringeth them up into an high mountain apart,

As mentioned earlier, days can and are very often translated or seen in the End Time revelation as years. And this is a great example. When this was revealed to me, I was at that point becoming very well versed in the revelation of the 14 years of the End Times. The easiest parts that caught my attention instantly were the, "**AFTER**" six days, in both Mark and Matthew. The first half of the 14 years for seals, which is Mark, the sleeping church. And the second half of the 14 years for Trumpets, which is Matthew, the Jews (also known as Jacob's trouble). So it was easy to understand these two right away.

This particular verse in Mark is a reference to the Lord coming at the end of or "after" the 6th seal, which is "**after**"6 years of Seals and the start of the 7th year sabbath. This is also the reason why we see Him coming at the end of the 6th seal. GOD's law has never changed, it has always been 6 and the 7th rest.

Matthew's verse of "**after"** 6 days is a reference to the Lord coming at the end of or "after" the 6th trumpet, which is "**after**" 6 years of Trumpets and the start of the 7th year sabbath. This is exactly when we see Him return feet down on the Mount of Olives, further confirmed in Revelation 11:15 that everything is now His, including all the kingdoms of the earth and reigning forever.

PS. A good side note here: Just because there are 6 seals over 6 years and 6 trumpets over 6 years, does not mean that the one seal or trumpet will only open up once the one before it has been completed, until all has been fulfilled. Some will happen close together, while others will happen in their time. Some will overlap, but have their biggest portion in their own time. And this also does not mean the Seal judgments will overlap with Trumpets either. Seals will be during their time and Trumpets will be during their time. We actually see this spoken about in the apocryphal book Baruch 2.

Luke's portion however, still remained a mystery to me for about a year, after having understood the other two of "after 6 days". I wanted to know why was Luke telling us, "about" an eight days? I was so excited when the Spirit revealed this mystery to me. It was perfect! This "about" was letting us know that it was not quite the 8th day/year. But it was close. And so, if you recall what you just read in the last section, you will get the answer.

> ***2 Corinthians 12:2***
> I knew a man in Christ **above** **fourteen years** ago, (whether in the body, I cannot tell; or whether out of the body, I cannot tell: God knoweth;) ***such an one*** **caught up** to the **third heaven**.

I knew the 14 years were those of Seals and Trumpets to Mark and Matthew. But there was this mysterious portion of time called "above" as we discussed earlier. The answer to this was the revelation of Luke's "about" an eight days. And just as Mark and Matthew's portions were coming at the end portion of Seals and Trumpets, this portion was then too coming after a period of time. And it either meant this portion of time was a little before the eight day/year or a little after it. But I already knew the tribulation was 7 total years for Seals and 7 total years for Trumpets. It had to mean this was a portion of time "**before**" the 14 years. Just as Paul was telling us in 2 Corinthians 12:2.

This meant a portion of time in the 7th day/year **before** the 8th began. We have also understood that the 8th day to GOD is also the first day of the week, of the next week. This would make that 8th day/year the first year of the 7 total years of Seals. Again confirming that it was **before** the 1st year that begins Seals, which is **"about"** an eighth day. It turned out to be exactly correct. This conversation in Luke's Transfiguration account with the "about" was the type and shadow of the period of time when the Son of Man will be coming for the 40 day warning, after the Escape of the Bride of Christ has happened, as you will have read in the chapter, *"Who Are The Gospels Speaking To?'* You will find greater understanding with regard to these 40 days when you come to the chapter, "*The 40 Days of The Son of Man*".

THE BIG PICTURE GIVEN IN THE STORY OF JACOB

> ***Genesis 31:41*** *(KJV)*
> Thus have I been **twenty years** in thy house; **I served thee fourteen years for thy two daughters**, **and six years** for thy cattle: and thou hast changed my wages ten times.

That is the end of the story. So let's back up a little to get the details of this story where Jacob worked for two daughters and cattle. In Genesis 29:18 we see Jacob loved Rachel and says he will work 7 years for her. Then in:

> ***Genesis 29:20*** *(KJV)*
> And Jacob served **7 years for Rachel** and they seemed unto him **but a few days**, for the love he had to her.

The reason for the first **7 years that seemed unto him but a few days,** was because of his love for her. So it is telling us that it was not really very hard on him, because he was excited. Time flew by! This is not the representation of the first 7 years of the 14 as some might be thinking. This first, what we have called "easy" 7 years, are the 7 years that the Holy Spirit has been working hard at preparing the bride of Christ. These are the 7 years that comes **before** the 14 years of tribulation begins. Meaning by the end of this first set of 7 years, the bride of Christ will be taken. As we continue we see in:

> ***Genesis 29:25*** *(KJV)*
> **25** And it came to pass, that in the morning, behold, it was Leah: and he said to Laban, What is this thou hast done unto me? Did not I serve with thee for Rachel? Wherefore then hast thou beguiled me?

Jacob, having completed 7 years, was expecting to get Rachel, the one he thought he was working for. However, he woke up the next morning to find out he was given the older sister, Leah, first. This is the type and shadow of when Jesus came in the New Testament and He said that He came, **"but unto the lost sheep of the house of Israel"** written in Matthew 15: 23 - 24. In this story of Jacob, the Gentile type and shadow is Leah.

> ***Matthew 15:23-28*** *(KJV)*
> **23** But he answered her not a word. And his disciples came and besought him, saying, Send her away; for she crieth after us.
> **24** But he answered and said, *I am not sent* ***but unto the lost sheep of the house of Israel*****.**

As the story continues we see this Gentile woman being referenced as a "dog". This was at that time as a Gentile reference. But then we see that because of her "great faith" her daughter is healed.

25 Then came she and worshipped him, saying,
Lord, help me.
26 But he answered and said, It is not meet to take
the children's bread, and to cast it to dogs.
27 And she said, Truth, Lord: yet the dogs eat of
the crumbs which fall from their masters' table.
28 Then Jesus answered and said unto her, O
woman, **great is thy faith**: be it unto thee even as
thou wilt. And her daughter was made whole from
that very hour.

We see that just as Jacob, Jesus had come for the one He really wanted, but the one He ended up getting were the Gentiles. The Gentiles who are grafted in for their faith in Him, while the vast majority of those He came for were not yet ready to accept or receive Him. As we read in:

Romans 11:11 and 22 - 24 *(KJV)*
11 I say then, Have they stumbled that they should
fall? God forbid: but rather through their fall
salvation is come unto the Gentiles, for to
provoke them to jealousy.
22 Behold therefore the goodness and severity of
God: on them which fell, severity; but toward thee,
goodness, if thou continue in his goodness:
otherwise thou also shalt be cut off.
23 And they also, *if they abide not still in unbelief,*
shall be grafted in: for God is able to graft them in
again.
24 For if thou wert cut out of the olive tree which is
wild by nature, **and wert grafted** contrary to
nature into a good olive tree: *how much more shall*

these, which be the natural branches, be grafted into their own olive tree?

Just as Jacob received the one he did not work / come for first, so did Christ. However, it was all of course according to GOD's perfect plan. It was by design that the Gentiles would be grafted in too. And this now brings us to the next part of this story.

Genesis 29:26 - 27 *(KJV)*
26 And Laban said, It must not be so done in our country, **to give the younger before the firstborn.**
27 Fulfil her week, and we will give thee this also for the service which thou shalt **serve with me *yet seven other years***.

We next see after he has realized that he received the other daughter, he goes to his father in law to confront him, who essentially says, "Too bad! Our tradition is the older one must be married off first." And then goes on to tell him, "**Fulfil her week**". This is a very special piece of scripture for the Luke group as the Bride of Christ. It is the representation of the Gentile wedding that will follow immediately the Escape, before the 7 years of Seals begins. But the group Jesus had originally come for, the house of Israel, the lost sheep that had been left behind as Mark's group, He will have to wait 7 years for. Jacob had to work the next 7 years to then fulfill her time. As we read at the end of verse 27... "for the service which thou shalt serve with me **yet seven more years"**.

Leaving the final years where Jacob remained to work for the cattle. As we read at the end of Genesis 31.

Genesis 31:41 (KJV)
41 ..***and six years*** *for thy cattle: and thou hast changed my wages ten times.*

These 6 years form the final years of his total 20 years. They are the representation of the final 6 years of Trumpets, or as most know it, "Jacob's Trouble", which brings us to a final piece of information in this story.

Genesis 31:44 *(KJV)*
44 Now therefore come thou, *let us* ***make a covenant***, I and thou; and let it be for a witness between me and thee.

CHAPTER 3

THE 40 DAYS OF THE SON OF MAN

This is a revelation of great importance. Even though you may possibly be reading this after it has happened. It will help protect you from the enemy who is to follow once you understand this. I will make it as clear as I can for those it may reach now and for those it will reach during that time. This period of time is not for the Bride of Christ. Luke's group, the bride of Christ, will have already been taken out of the earth as per -

> ***Acts 15:14*** *(KJV)*
> **14** Simeon hath declared how God at the first did visit the Gentiles, to take out of them a people for his name.

Only days before this time of the Son of Man begins.

It is not an easy subject to share, because most have never understood that there is more than one event relating to the Lord in the End Times. You will see that there is much more involved than Him simply returning feet down on the Mount of Olives at the end. And it will start with this.

It all begins with a portion of time that our Brother Paul tells us about in:

> ***2 Corinthians 12:2*** *(KJV)*
> **2** "I knew a man in Christ "**ABOVE**" 14 years ago... "

We are looking at what this "<u>above</u>" portion Paul is referring to. First of all, it must be less than 15 years or he would have said, above 15 years. The mystery of it is **how much** "<u>above</u>" the 14 years and what takes place during that time. And in fact, you will see wording a little later on that shows Jesus knew this would not be widely understood about Him at this time.

But why is it so crazy or difficult to believe when it is repeatedly spoken about in scripture, from Noah to Jonah to the Lord Himself? The understanding will come from all three of the synoptic gospels. And yet, whenever we discuss this, most instantly see us as heretical and twisting scripture. When we are actually comparing scripture with scripture as the Word tells us to do. Having read and begun to understand who the gospels are speaking to, you can now do the same with much more clarity. You are about to understand for yourself that it is a downright fact -***<u>The Son of Man is coming for 40 Days,</u>*** first or above/before the 14 years begin!

I know many may right now say, "But Jesus told us not to believe people that would be saying they are Christ coming in His name", quoting these scriptures below.

> ***Matthew 24:5*** *(KJV)*
> **5** For many <u>shall come in my name, **saying**, I am Christ</u>; and shall deceive many.

Or how about

Mark 13:6 *(KJV)*
6 For many shall come in my name, **saying**, I am Christ; and shall deceive many.

And how about

Luke 21:8 *(KJV)*
8 And he said, Take heed that ye be not deceived: for many shall come in my name, **saying**, I am Christ; and the time draweth near: go ye not therefore after them.

What do they all have in common? "*shall come in my name, **saying, I am Christ***". Let me ask you, when Christ was here before and after His resurrection, did He go around telling everyone He was the Christ? No, He did not. Here are a couple of examples -

Luke 9:18-19 *(KJV)*
18 And it came to pass, as he was alone praying, his disciples were with him: and he asked them, saying, Whom say the people that I am?
19 They answering said, John the Baptist; but some say, Elias; and others say, that one of the old prophets is risen again.

Matthew 16:15-17 *(KJV)*
15 He saith unto them, But whom say ye that I am?
16 And Simon Peter answered and said, Thou art the Christ, the Son of the living God.
17 And Jesus answered and said unto him, Blessed art thou, Simon Barjona: ***for flesh and blood hath***

not revealed it unto thee, *but my Father which is in heaven.*

In both of these cases, as the others found in scripture, He never went around telling them He was the Christ. Clearly in Luke's account here, if He had, He would not have asked the question. More to the point, they obviously did not know by all the answers He got. In fact, in Matthew's account we see the only way any of them could have known He really was the Christ, was if it was the will of the Father in heaven that they were given to understand it. Not because He told them.

People came to believe He was, but never do we read of Jesus going around to groups of people telling them He was the Christ. The declaring in itself is the very difference that brings us clarity. Proving that all who have declared to be in the past and all who will in the future, are not the Christ. He did not and will not be going around telling everyone He is the Christ. It is important to remember this. Saying and proving that He will be here for 40 days is not contradicting those scriptures. It is bringing clarity to what they really mean.

WHAT SIGN IS "JONAH" AND WHEN?

For generations people have argued that there are contradictions in the scriptures. This is one of those they debate. It is the story of Jonah given to us in the gospels. Let's have a look.

LUKE

Luke 11:29-30 *(KJV)*
29 ...they seek a sign; and *there shall no sign be given it*, **but** the sign of Jonas the prophet.

30 For **as Jonas was a sign** unto the Ninevites, **so shall also the Son of man be** to this generation.

MARK

Mark 8:12-13 *(KJV)*
12 Why doth this generation seek after a sign? verily I say unto you, *There shall no sign be given* ***unto this generation***.
13 And he left them, and entering into the ship again departed to the other side.

MATTHEW

Matthew 12:39-30 *(KJV)*
39 ...and *there shall no sign be given to it*, **but** the sign of the prophet Jonas:
40 For **as Jonas was three days and three nights** in the whale's belly; **so shall the Son of man be** three days and three nights **in the heart of the earth**.

Right away we can clearly see where the argument is for the contradiction, especially in Mark, the one debated most. How is it that Jesus said he would be as Jonah, in Luke and Matthew, yet in Mark tells them, "No sign will be given" and gets in a ship and leaves? It is not just that Mark is told nothing. There is more going on here. There is also that Luke is told one portion and Matthew another portion. And exactly what did He mean in Luke by, He will be **a sign** as Jonah was?

We have all heard the term, "Was, and Is, and Is to Come" being taught. "Was" as the scripture history of it, "is" as the life lessons for us to take from scripture, and the "is to come" as it would apply to the End Times. However, there is even more to this than what we have been taught all along with regard to the subject of the Son of Man being here for 40 days. Luke's version in this case will represent the "was" (pre-tribulation or before the 14 years, but after the escape). Mark, the "is" (mid-tribulation/rapture), and Matthew, the "is to come" (post-tribulation/feet down).

The way we have always been taught to understand it was Matthew's portion represented the 3 days after His crucifixion to His resurrection and that the 40 days after His resurrection was Luke's portion. However, Jesus told us in Luke's version that He would be as Jonah was. What did Jonah do during his 40 days? He gave them a **warning** of what was about to happen to them if they did not heed his words and repent. So that would mean Jesus did not yet do as Jonah did His first time around. Sure He had a 40 day event, but He did not do as Jonah did, like He said He would in Luke 11. And now you can begin to understand that He still actually has to fulfil a 40 day warning.

The focus of this chapter is the 40 days of the Son of Man. However, I feel like I would be leaving you hanging without at least touching on the understanding of why Mark and Matthew's versions speak differently of their

Jonah story. So I am going to try and cover just the main points of them. Let's start with Mark and the reason he is told no sign. As we have come to understand, the end of Mark's portion is <u>after</u> the 6 years of Seals and what or who do we see coming at the end of the 6th seal?

> ***Revelation 6:16*** *(KJV)*
> **16** And said to the mountains and rocks, Fall on us, and <u>hide us</u> **from the face of him that sitteth on the throne**, <u>and from the wrath of the Lamb</u>:

What can we understand from this? That there was no warning or no sign given before His sudden appearing. This is the understanding of the end of Mark's time and it is in the exact place in the End Times it should be to relate to Mark's "no sign".

Matthew's portion of three days and three nights could be a big discussion, because it is a huge revelation. But I will keep it short. We have all been told that Jesus was three days and three nights in the grave. Many of you may know this has caused a lot of confusion in the church as to how could Jesus have then risen early in the morning on the first day of the week after a Passover crucifixion and it be after three days and three nights? The answer is, it could not have! And this opens another very big discussion. Seeing that it clearly shows that it is not, how is it we have all been taught this for generations? The short answer is that we have all been taught from the perspective of Matthew's gospel and only used Mark and Luke's gospels as a backup support to build on the view from Matthew, instead of incorporating and dividing the word, comparing scripture with scripture. As you have come to understand, they are not just another perspective, but completely different groups of people spoken to. Now there are many verses I can use to show that it was not after three days and three nights, but here is three.

> ***Luke 24:46*** *(KJV)*
> **46** And said unto them, Thus it is written, and thus it behoved Christ to suffer, and to rise from the dead **the third day**:
>
> ***1 Corinthians 15:3-4*** *(KJV)*
> **3** For I delivered unto you first of all that which I also received, how that Christ died for our sins according to the scriptures;
>
> **4** And that he was buried, and that he rose again **the third day** according to the scriptures:
>
> ***Matthew 17:22-23*** *(KJV)*
> **22** And while they abode in Galilee, Jesus said unto them, The Son of man shall be betrayed into the hands of men:
> **23** And they shall kill him, and the third day he shall be raised again. And they were exceeding sorry.

Clearly if it was after three days and three nights He would have had to rise from the dead on the fourth day? Yet not one of them tells us this and there are many more scriptures that say the same thing. So where did this come from? In one place in Matthew's gospel, the Jonah story, even though every other scripture told us He rose **on the third day** and not after. So this leaves the question. Why did Jesus say He would be as Jonah was for three days and three nights? Well just as Luke and Mark were speaking prophetically of something that was in the "is to come", so too was Matthew's Jonah account. When you read carefully the Matthew verses above, you will see what was really being told to us about the time of His death and resurrection. It tells us from when He will be betrayed into the hands of men, which would be the beginning of the count, then it goes on to say they will kill Him, and finally, on the third Day He will be raised. This is how He was able to rise on the first day of the week early in the morning and still have it be on the third day! It was never the total time in the grave at His death and resurrection. It began from when He was taken. Hence, clearly He was not, nor could have been in the grave for three days and three nights, let alone also count the time of His crucifixion. Leaving one truth... "is to come". The details to that discussion will not be happening in this book.

Now moving back into the 40 day conversation. Let's look at a very telling piece of scripture that will again not only shed more light on the 40 days, but also give more about Mark and Matthew's times.

Luke 17:24 - 30 *(KJV)*
24 For as the lightning, that lighteneth out of the one part under heaven, shineth unto the other part under heaven; *so shall also the Son of man be in his* ***day****.*
25 **But first** *must he suffer many things, and be rejected of* **this *generation*.**
26 And as it was in the days of Noe, *so shall it be*

*also in the **days** of the Son of man.*
27 They did eat, they drank, they married wives,
they were given in marriage, **until** the day that Noe
entered into the ark, and the flood came, and
destroyed them all.
28 Likewise also as it was in the days of Lot; they
did eat, they drank, **they bought, they sold**, they
planted, they builded;
29 But the same day that Lot went out of Sodom it
rained fire and brimstone from heaven, and
destroyed them all.
30 Even thus shall it be in the day when the Son of
Man **is revealed.**

Now again, the Mark and Matthew portions are not the point of this teaching. However, I am going to quickly show them to you. Then move into Luke's 40 day portion and show you where it leads us to from there.

In **Luke 17:24** you will notice He starts by telling them the end when He will return feet down on the Mount of Olives as lighting from one end to the other, which we now understand is the end of the 6th trumpet time. And how do we know? He tells them His "day" will be like lightning from one part of heaven to the other. This is Matthew's portion. This is also the scripture people quote to say that there will not be a "secret escape", because the whole world will see Him when He comes. But as you have also now come to understand, they say this only because they are seeing it from a Matthew perspective and have not understood Mark or Luke's perspective. So how can we know how this is to the end at His feet down return? Remember Matthew's portion is Trumpets time to the end.

> ***Matthew 24: 27*** *(KJV)*
> **27** For **as the lightning cometh** out of the east, and shineth even unto the west; so shall also the **coming of the Son of Man be**.

You will also remember that in 2 Corinthians 12:14, Paul, as a type and shadow of Jesus Christ, says that it is the third time and that he will be **coming to them.**

Now if we skip to Luke 17:28, because I want to show Mark's portion before getting to Luke's, you will notice some very interesting words - "they bought, they sold". Interesting how that wording is found in that portion. Remember, a big focus during the tribulation of Seals is going to be having or not having the ability to "buy or sell", due to the mark of the beast. When you continue down to verse 30, you will notice it says "when the Son of Man is **revealed**". This is not the 40 days, nor His return feet down on the Mount of Olives, but the time when He will come after the 6th seal. As we read in -

> ***Revelation 6:16 -17*** *(KJV)*
> **16** And said to the mountains and rocks, Fall on us, and *hide us from the face of him that sitteth on the throne,* ***and from the wrath of the Lamb***:
> **17** *For the great day of his wrath is come; and who shall be able to stand?*

This is when He will be seen coming on Mount Zion as the great stone that will become a mountain, seen here:

Daniel 2:34-35 *(KJV)*
34 Thou sawest till that a stone was cut out
without hands, which smote the image upon his
feet that were of iron and clay, and brake them to
pieces.
35 Then was the iron, the clay, the brass, the silver,
and the gold, broken to pieces together, and
became like the chaff of the summer threshing
floors; and the wind carried them away, that no
place was found for them: and the stone that smote
the image **became a great mountain**, and filled
the whole earth.

The end of Mark's time of tribulation! This is when Lord will destroy the beast and his system shortly before the coming rapture of Mark's group.

So in verse 24 it is the End of Trumpets, Matthew's time, which He tells them about first, and verse 28, it is the end of Seals, Mark's. Now we will look at Luke's time, the 40 days of the Son of Man.

Let me add a little context to rightly divide these few verses. The context of these verses in Luke 17 is about His coming Kingdom. They are asking Him, "Is it now, how will we know?" And He goes on to tell them about it. He tells them what it is going to be like when the end is approaching. He is not telling them anything about the time they are presently in. He is clearly giving them prophecy, because that was not yet the time of His Kingdom.

Now you will notice in **Luke 17:25** after He has told them the Matthew portion when He will come as lightning in

His day, says some very important words - "**But First**", which means, **before**. He is saying before these things I have just told you about (when He will come as lighting in His day), I am going to have to suffer many things and be rejected.

And so what is this "But first"? In verse 26 He says that His "day**S**" will be as the "day**s**" of Noah. In verse 24, the Matthew section, it was his DAY, singular, but here in verse 26 it is plural. The question is, which "day**S"** could those be? First it confirms the fact that this is another portion of time, besides the obvious "But first". And He is also telling us in verse 27 that His "day**S**" that He will be here for, relate to Noah. He gives us a clue with the reference to Noah, which tells us exactly how many day**s** they are by telling us it was "**until**" Noah got in the ark and the flood came. And how long was this time? You got it, *40 days*! Let's go to the story itself and see what He is referring to. Also remembering that the End Time context we are looking at is a portion of time called "above" the 14 years, which simply means **before** the tribulation actually starts. As a side note, this does not mean that it will not be a crazy time that has begun on the earth. It most certainly will be. However, it will not yet be the beginning of the 14 years quite yet, until after the "above or before" portion has ended.

This story of Noah and the ark is given to us in Genesis 7 and 8. We see GOD telling Noah in **Genesis 7:4** For yet seven days, and I will cause it to rain upon the earth forty days and forty nights. And we see he starts gathering in his family and the animals. By verse 10 the seven days have passed and the flood has begun.

Genesis 7:10 *(KJV)*
10 And it came to pass **after** seven days, that the waters of the flood were upon the earth.

At this point the 40 days have started. Now let's go to the main part of this story that Jesus is referring us to from Luke 17 to understand His connection to the 40 days being "before" or "above" 14 years, and right before the tribulation begins.

Genesis 8:6-13 *(KJV)*
6 And it came to pass at **the end of forty days**,
that Noah opened the window of the ark which he
had made:
7 And he sent forth a raven, which went forth to
and fro, until the waters were dried up from off the
earth.
8 *Also* he sent forth **a dove** from him, to see if the
waters were abated from off the face of the ground;
9 But the dove found no rest for the sole of her
foot, and she returned unto him into the ark, for the
waters were on the face of the whole earth: then he
put forth his hand, and took her, and pulled her in
unto him into the ark.
10 And he **stayed** yet other **seven days**; and again
he sent forth the dove out of the ark;
11 And the dove came in to him in the evening;
and, lo, in her mouth was **an olive leaf pluckt off**:
so Noah knew that the waters were abated from off
the earth.
12 And he **stayed** yet other **seven days**; and sent
forth the dove; **which returned not again** unto
him any more.

13 And it came to pass in the six hundredth and first year, in the first month, the first day of the month, the waters were dried up from off the earth: and Noah removed the covering of the ark.

As you by now know, the tribulation time of Seals and Trumpets is 14 years. And did you notice that "after" the 40 days, we read in verses 10 and 12 **Seven** days and **Seven** days? Let's look at Mark's portion first. You will notice this first 7 days, as a type and shadow of years, has passed in verse 10, when the dove returns. Except only this time it has an olive leaf/branch "**pluckt**" off. This is the representation of the end of Mark's portion at the end of Seals, rapture. Let's see what the meaning of the word rapture is, or more specifically, for this one we read in 2 Corinthians 12:4... "was caught up"

It is the Greek word **G726 Harpazo**, meaning, catch (away, up), **pluck**.

Or ***pluckt*** as we just saw after the first 7, after the 40 days. Fitting is it not? And consider also that we are told the Gentiles were "grafted in" as a wild olive branch into the true olive tree. The dove came back with a **"pluckt"** off olive "**leaf (H5929)**". And to be sure let's see what this word leaf means.

Leaf **(H5929)** a leaf (as coming up on a tree); collectively foliage: - **branch**, leaf.

Here is what Romans tells us about this "branch".

Romans 11:17 *(KJV)*
17 And if some of the branches be broken off, and thou, being a wild olive tree, wert grafted in among

them, and with them partakest of the root and fatness of the olive tree;

So you can see why the dove after this first 7 days/years has the olive leaf/ branch "**pluckt** off". It represents the end of Seals and the church age at MARK's mid-tribulation rapture.

As for Matthew's portion, we read in verse 12 that the dove goes out again after its second 7 and it returns no more, showing us clearly that this is now the end of tribulation. The 14 days/years are over, being the end of Matthew's portion. So let's go see what the last chapter of Matthew tells us.

Matthew 28:18-20 *(KJV)*
18 And Jesus came and spake unto them, saying,
All power is given unto me in heaven and in earth.
19 Go ye therefore, and teach all nations, baptizing
them in the name of the Father, and of the Son, and
of the Holy Ghost:
20 Teaching them to observe all things whatsoever
I have commanded you: *and, lo,* **I am with you
always, *even unto the end of the world.*** Amen.

He will now remain on earth with them until the end of it, which is at the end of Trumpets, to the end of the world at the end of the 1000 year reign.

Where do we find the 40 days going back to the beginning of this story, Paul tells us in 2 Corinthians 12:2 "Above" 14 years ago. Just like Jesus clearly tells us in Luke 17:25 "But First". Telling us that His day"**S**" will be 40 as Noah's, that they will come "first", and will be "before" the 14 years of tribulation, and during those 40 days He will do as Jonah did, warn the people! Unfortunately, He then also tells us that during this time He will be rejected.

Let's continue to build on the dove and its type and shadow in the Noah story. We find the first account of the Holy Ghost/Dove in the New Testament in Acts 2. This was after the 40 days of the Son of Man has just ended from Acts 1, after His resurrection. In the Old Testament the first place the Dove shows up is in Genesis 8:8 and we just showed how it is representing the same type and shadow of the Pentecost story, which is the time frame of the Holy Ghost after the 40 days of the flood portion, to the Dove. So let's look closer to see what this storyline from the New Testament tells us.

Old testament Noah's flood:

- Family saved
- 40 days
- Short time to sending out the dove (50th day), then the dove returns to ark.
- 7 days/years, dove goes and returns, with "pluckt" leaf/branch.
- 7 days/years, dove sent out and never returns.

End Times:

- Escape of the Bride, Luke.
- 40 days of the Son of man, Luke 24 after His resurrection.

- Short time to sending out the Holy Ghost/Dove (50th day), then Holy Ghost returns to heaven, Acts 2.
- Tribulation begins with the first 7 years, Seals and then "rapture" of the "grafted in branch", Mark.
- Second 7 years, Trumpets, and the Lord returns never leaving again, Matthew.

**Please see for easy reference the 14 Year Timeline Chart in the Appendix at the back of the book.*

THE RESURRECTION

On a final note in the synoptic gospels, I want to show you one last beautiful type and shadow of the Lord's Bride, His Body, that yet again lets us know she is taken before the 40 days of the Son of Man's warning and that it truly is Luke that is representing her in his gospel, here in the resurrection story. You see very different and specific wording in Luke than you do in the other two -

LUKE

> ***Luke 24:3-4*** *(KJV)*
> **3** And they entered in, and found not **the body** of the Lord Jesus.
> **4** And it came to pass, as they were much perplexed thereabout, behold, two men stood by them in shining garments:

MARK

> ***Mark 16:5*** *(KJV)*
> **5** And entering into the sepulchre, they saw a

young man sitting on the right side, clothed in a
long white garment; and they were affrighted.

MATTHEW

Matthew 28:2-3 *(KJV)*
2 And, behold, there was a great earthquake: for
the angel of the Lord descended from heaven, and
came and rolled back the stone from the door, and
sat upon it.
3 His countenance was like lightning, and his
raiment white as snow:

You will notice it was only Luke's gospel that said, His **"BODY"** ***was not found***. Considering everything being revealed in connection to His coming 40 days and that the Bride of Christ/His Body must be removed *before* His 40 days begin, you can see why **THE BODY** WAS NOT FOUND. And what *followed and will follow* the resurrection of the Bride this time? You got it... the Son of Man's 40 days.

In this next portion, called "A Word of Caution", the caution is not the understanding of the 40 days, but to caution because of the source. It is not from scripture, however it is so relevant I felt I had no choice but to share it with you and explain it.

A WORD OF CAUTION
(THAT GIVES GREATER EVIDENCE)

As great a place that might have been to end this topic, I want to put forth one more piece of evidence. It is not from the Bible. It comes from one of the enemy's playbooks. I like to share this whenever I talk about the

40 days of the Son of Man, because it is quite eye opening. Some will even say, "Why is it in one of the enemy's books and not given so clearly in our own?" The answer is the Bible has clearly told us, as you have just read. However, the issue it will always come back to, as to why it was not until now, is we have all been taught to understand from the perspective of Matthew's gospel. And it has caused us to miss more than half of the understanding in the End Time story.

As for my answer to your question, "Why so clearly in the enemy's books?". I believe the enemy has told them ahead of time, in the hopes that he does not lose any to the truth, when the Son of Man does come and is performing many incredible miracles during those days. Remember what Jesus said in Luke 17:25 about this time.

Let's go to Jesus' own words again in:

> ***Luke 17:25*** *(KJV)*
> **25** <u>**But first** must he suffer many things, **and be rejected of this generation**</u>.

So what evidence do we have from one of the enemy's books that I like to share? It is the story of the coming of "The Dajjal". The Muslims call the Dajjal, the Christian antichrist. And from what I have just explained about the Son of Man coming for 40 days, and how people are still holding onto those scriptures that say many will come in <u>My Name</u>, it is easy to see how Jesus will in fact be rejected of this generation. As you will see, He clearly is not the Christian antichrist, but most will not understand, because the sleeping church, left behind, was taught that antichrist comes first. How can we know for sure that this really is not the antichrist? The easy answer is that it is in one of their books for starters, and they are calling Him the antichrist.

First let me share with you the main points of this person compared to their "two guys" coming after him. They say this Dajjal person will be here for 40 days.

> "We asked: How long will he remain on the earth? He replied: Forty days."
>
> And that he will be doing so many incredible miracles which include:
>
> Such as healing the sick, raising the dead (although only when supported by his demonic followers it seems), causing the earth to grow vegetation, causing livestock to prosper and to die and stopping the sun's movement.[6] *His miracles resemble* ***those performed by Jesus***. *The relation between the two is obscure*."

This is all literally written about this Dajjal person found in one of their books. This information is from https://en.wikipedia.org/wiki/Al-Masih_ad-Dajjal, the "Wikipedia Dajjal page".

They say he will be doing such incredible miracles that it will be hard to distinguish between what Jesus did when He was here, and what this person will do. Christians have been taught to believe that the antichrist will come first, when in fact Jesus, as the Son of Man, will be here first for 40 days!

And they go on to say that "their two people" who will come after, will be the "real" Jesus, but in reality will be the biblical false prophet, and the other will be their Mahdi, who will be the actual antichrist. They say their "real" Jesus will go after this Dajjal person (our Jesus Messiah) and get rid of him! And then their Mahdi will rule for either 6, 7 or 9 years. We know here that this rule will be more like 6 years, during the Seals portion before the rapture of Mark's group in the 7th year Sabbath of Seals.

Are you now seeing why the Son of Man will be rejected? The Left Behind church has no idea who He will be and sadly most of them will reject Him too. Now you see how confused the church is and why this is so important. Everyone out there is saying that it is 7 years and the antichrist will come first. Although the antichrist does show up around the start of the 14 years, ***he does not come first!***

I cannot stress enough how important it is that we understand this revelation of *Jesus in Luke 17* and Luke 11. He, Jesus, as the Son of Man, will be here for 40 days to warn the people, even in the midst of rejection *again,* "before" the antichrist comes on the scene.

Please note that although He will be rejected, there will be some that come to Him believing and knowing who He is. They will become His Apostles and Disciples. These will be those who will receive the End Time "Acts 2.0" as we call it, the Holy Ghost anointing on the 50th day to lead the great End Time revival during the tribulation of Seals.

Now is the time to seek Him and take comfort in Him, knowing that His Bride will not take part in any of this. For those reading this shortly after His Bride has been taken, tens of millions of people having vanished, know that the first person on the scene giving warning and doing incredible miracles IS the Son of Man fulfilling His 40 days Warning! And for those after this period of time, when the Son of Man is gone, know and understand that the two, who will shortly after come on the scene, ARE the antichrist (Mahdi) and the false prophet, who they will call Jesus. Do not follow them at any cost. Call out to Jesus Christ, repent and ask Him to forgive you all your sins and to guide you in this time in His will. I promise He will hear you!

PSALM 38

1 O LORD, rebuke me not in thy wrath: neither chasten me in thy hot displeasure.

2 For thine arrows stick fast in me, and thy hand presseth me sore.

3 *There is* no soundness in my flesh because of thine anger; neither *is there any* rest in my bones because of my sin.

4 For mine iniquities are gone over mine head: as an heavy burden they are too heavy for me.

5 My wounds stink *and* are corrupt because of my foolishness.

6 I am troubled; I am bowed down greatly; I go mourning all the day long.

7 For my loins are filled with a loathsome *disease*: and *there is* no soundness in my flesh.

8 I am feeble and sore broken: I have roared by reason

of the disquietness of my heart.
9 Lord, all my desire *is* before thee; and my groaning is
not hid from thee.
10 My heart panteth, my strength faileth me: as for the
light of mine eyes, it also is gone from me.
11 My lovers and my friends stand aloof from my sore;
and my kinsmen stand afar off.
12 They also that seek after my life lay snares *for me*:
and they that seek my hurt speak mischievous things,
and imagine deceits all the day long.
13 But I, as a deaf *man*, heard not; and *I was* as a dumb
man *that* openeth not his mouth.
14 Thus I was as a man that heareth not, and in whose
mouth *are* no reproofs.
15 For in thee, O LORD, do I hope: thou wilt hear, O
Lord my God.
16 For I said, *Hear me*, lest *otherwise* they should
rejoice over me: when my foot slippeth, they magnify
themselves against me.
17 For I *am* ready to halt, and my sorrow *is* continually
before me.
18 For I will declare mine iniquity; I will be sorry for my
sin.
19 But mine enemies *are* lively, *and* they are strong:
and they that hate me wrongfully are multiplied.
20 They also that render evil for good are mine
adversaries; because I follow *the thing that* good *is*.
21 Forsake me not, O LORD: O my God, be not far from
me.
22 Make haste to help me, O Lord my salvation.

CHAPTER 4

THE REVELATION OF DANIEL 9

I would like to start out by saying I am not going to be speaking about what "was". Meaning I am not proving out the count of Daniel 9 to when Jesus came the first time, even though it was incomplete. This study is the revelation of the "Is To Come". And you will see the confusion and misunderstanding in the wording that has been taught by churches for so long, including that famous verse 27 everyone likes to go to. This has been something that truly needed clarifying.

We are not going to go into detail on all of Daniel 9. Our focus will be on the very famous portion Daniel 9:24-27. Let's start by first reading it all.

> ***Daniel 9:24-27*** *(KJV)*
> **24 Seventy weeks** (**H7620**) are determined upon
> thy people and upon thy holy city, to finish the
> transgression, and to make an end of sins, and to
> make reconciliation for iniquity, and to bring in
> everlasting righteousness, and to seal up the vision
> and prophecy, and to anoint the most Holy.
> **25** Know therefore and understand, that from the
> going forth of **the commandment** (H1697) ***to***
> ***restore and to build Jerusalem*** unto the Messiah
> the **P**rince shall be **seven weeks**, and ***threescore***
> ***and two weeks***: *the street shall be built again, and*
> *the wall*, even in troublous times.
> **26** And **after** threescore and two weeks shall

Messiah be **cut off**, but not for himself: and the people of the **p**rince that shall come shall ***destroy the city and the sanctuary***, and the end thereof shall be with **a flood**, and unto the ***end of the war*** desolations are determined.
27 And **he** shall *confirm the covenant with many* for **one week**: and in the midst of the week **he** shall cause the sacrifice and the oblation to cease, and for the overspreading of abominations **he shall make it desolate**, even until the consummation, and that determined shall be poured upon the desolate.

I do not want to get too caught up in the understanding or revelation of the "Seventy/70 weeks" that starts verse 24. However, there is great importance in truly understanding where the end of 70 years is according to the LORD GOD. Throughout scripture from Daniel to Jeremiah, to Zechariah and many more, all tell us of the 70 years. That is why I do need to make a couple points regarding it, because we need this understanding to form the foundation of what is to follow.

This is that Israel came into the land that the Lord gave them again almost 2000 years later in May of 1948, which means that the 70th year of Israel having been in the land came to an end in May of 2018. For a while many have spoken about the 70th year of Israel being a sure sign to look for the coming of the Lord. However, as you know, Israel's "70th year" has come and gone. Did God make a mistake? No. What many failed to see was a **very important** scripture in Leviticus 19: 23 - 24 that reveals why it was in fact not then. GOD tells us that they were not to count or begin from day one when they came into the land He would give them, but He tells them to wait.

> ***Leviticus 19:23-24*** *(KJV)*
> **23** And **when ye shall come into the land**, and shall have planted all manner of trees for food, then ye shall count the fruit thereof as uncircumcised: ***three years*** shall it be as uncircumcised unto you: it shall not be eaten of.
> **24** But in the fourth year all the fruit thereof shall be holy to praise the LORD withal.

According to this scripture, when they came into the land in May 1948, they were not to take from the land for three years, which they did not do. This would then make it May 1948 + 3 years = May 1951 in which the three years would then have been completed. From the time of the 4th year, GOD then said it "shall be holy to praise the LORD withal". So May 1951 + 70 years gives us the end of the 70th year, May 2021!

The second point is on the word "weeks". When reading this in the End Time understanding we cannot look at it as times 7 x 7 weeks count as it "was" understood to be the first time Jesus came. The churches have tried to carry forward this way of counting it into the End Times understanding, but it cannot be done. It has only brought confusion. Remember, we are not looking at what "was", but what "is to come".

At a closer look at the word "weeks", we see it means; shâbûaʽ, which represents the Feast of Weeks or as most of us know it by, Pentecost, just as we read in Leviticus 23.

Leviticus 23:15-17 *(KJV)*

15 And ye shall count unto you from the morrow after the sabbath, from the day that ye brought the sheaf of the wave offering; *seven sabbaths shall be complete:*

16 *Even unto the morrow after the seventh sabbath shall ye number* ***fifty days***, and ye shall offer a new meat offering unto the LORD.

17 Ye shall bring out of your habitations two wave loaves of two tenth deals: they shall be of fine flour; *they shall be baken* ***with leaven***; ***they are the firstfruits*** *unto the LORD*.

We get the understanding here, but we are missing the word definition for Feast of Weeks. For that we will have go to -

Exodus 34:22 *(KJV)*

22 And thou shalt observe ***the feast of weeks*** **(H7620)**, of **the firstfruits** of wheat harvest, and the feast of ingathering at the year's end.

H7620 - **shâbûaʿ**, shaw-boo'-ah; or שָׁבֻעַ shâbuaʿ; also (feminine) שְׁבֻעָה shᵉbuʿâh; properly, passive participle of H7650 as a denominative of H7651; literally, sevened, i.e. a week (specifically, of years):—seven, week.

This is telling us the Feast of Weeks is shâbûaʿ. Let me emphasize that we are not looking at this to say times 7. We are reading it for what it is directly saying and that is, ***"70"*** Feast of Weeks. What is to happen **"after"** these

70 Feasts of Weeks/ Pentecosts/ Years have come to an end? The answer lies in verses 25 - 27.

> ***Daniel 9:25*** (KJV)
> **25** Know therefore and understand, that from the going forth of **the commandment (H1697)** ***to restore and to build Jerusalem***...

We see in this verse that there is a "commandment" given to start to restore/rebuild Jerusalem. From this we can see that Israel will be attacked and destroyed first in order to be rebuilt, which as mentioned earlier, is explained in the middle verses of the chapter. An important question we should ask is, "Who makes this commandment/decree/declaration (H1697)?" For that we go to -

> ***2 Chronicles 36:21-23*** *(KJV)*
> **21** To fulfil the word of the LORD by the mouth of
> Jeremiah, until the land had enjoyed her sabbaths:
> for as long as she lay **desolate** she kept sabbath, to
> fulfil **threescore and ten years.**
> **22** *Now in the first year of* ***Cyrus king of Persia***,
> that the word of the LORD spoken by the mouth of
> Jeremiah might be accomplished, the LORD stirred
> up the spirit of **Cyrus king of Persia**, *that he made*
> ***a proclamation*** throughout all his kingdom, and
> put it also in writing, saying,
> **23** Thus saith **Cyrus king of Persia**, All the
> kingdoms of the earth hath the LORD God of
> heaven given me; and *he hath charged me to build*
> *him an house in Jerusalem*, which is in Judah. Who

is there among you of all his people? The LORD his God be with him, and let him go up.

We see here the 70 years again as the "threescore and ten years" and that the land is going to lay desolate for a period of time so that "the land enjoyed her sabbaths". These words of "the land enjoyed her sabbaths" are very important to our End Time understanding. And finally we see that Cyrus is the one who made the "decree/ commandment to rebuild". What is this period of time for "sabbath/rest that she is to enjoy" and why? Remember we are looking at this in how it relates to this period of the End Times that is just about to begin on the earth. Let's consider the "now" of it. Since Israel has captured Jerusalem, it has been a little over 50 years. And in that time, has Israel ever once allowed the land to rest? The answer is no! This "rest" was commanded and written in God's law.

Leviticus 25:3-5 *(KJV)*
3 Six years thou shalt sow thy field, and six years thou shalt prune thy vineyard, and gather in the fruit thereof;
4 *But in* ***the seventh year shall be a sabbath of rest unto the land****,* a sabbath for the LORD: thou shalt neither sow thy field, nor prune thy vineyard.
5 That which growth of its own accord of thy harvest thou shalt not reap, neither gather the grapes of thy vine undressed: ***for it is a year of rest unto the land.***

This is telling us that every 7th year was to be a time of rest for the land and they were not to plant or harvest it.

They were to rely on GOD that He would provide their needs in obedience. This was to continue every 7th year they were in the land, in particular Jerusalem. They are told in the following verses that they were to continue doing this every 7th year, for 7 years for a total of 49 years. The 50th year would be a special time called the Jubilee year.

> ***Leviticus 25:8-10*** *(KJV)*
> **8** And thou shalt <u>number seven sabbaths of years</u>
> unto thee, seven times seven years; and <u>the space</u>
> <u>of the seven sabbaths of years **shall be unto thee**</u>
> <u>**forty and nine years**</u>.
> **9** Then shalt thou cause the trumpet of **the jubilee**
> to sound on the tenth day of the seventh month, in
> the day of atonement shall ye make the trumpet
> sound throughout all your land.
> **10** And ye shall hallow **the fiftieth year**, and
> <u>*proclaim liberty throughout all the land unto all the*</u>
> <u>*inhabitants thereof*</u>: it shall be a jubilee unto you;
> and <u>*ye shall return every man unto his possession,*</u>
> <u>*and ye shall return every man unto his family*</u>.

Again, this is not something they have observed since capturing Jerusalem. Is GOD only going to shrug His shoulders and say, "Oh well..." to this disobedience? They of all people should have known better. God does not change. Judgment comes to the house of the LORD first. The Lord commanded the land to rest.

Now that we know what was required of them concerning the land, what does scripture tell us would happen should they not be obedient in this commandment?

Leviticus 26:32-35 *(KJV)*
32 And I will bring the land into desolation: and your enemies which dwell therein shall be astonished at it.
33 And I will scatter you among the heathen, and will draw out a sword after you: and **your land shall be desolate**, and your cities waste.
34 Then shall ***the land enjoy her sabbaths***, as long as it lieth desolate, and ye be in your enemies' land; ***even then shall the land rest, and enjoy her sabbaths.***
35 As long as it lieth desolate it shall rest; ***because it did not rest in your sabbaths, when ye dwelt upon it.***

How much more clear does it have to be? Also, remember that 2 Chronicles 36:21 told us this period was related to 70 years and that Cyrus would come to power and be the one to make this "decree".

When we go back to Daniel 9:25, we can see and understand why what follows the decree is a portion of time called "7 weeks/feast of weeks", or as we now know "7 years", is mentioned. It has to do with their failure to have observed the sabbath years once every 7 years since having Jerusalem. Now the land will take her rest as per GOD's law, only through judgment by destroying the land. We have heard countless reports that Israel is about to build the Third Temple, but from what we have just read and come to understand, GOD cannot allow it to be built on His land, **until the land has had her appointed rest for 7 Years.**

The second part of verse 25 tells us,

> ***Daniel 9:25*** *(KJV)*
> **25 … , and** threescore and two weeks: ***the street shall be built again, and the wall***, even in troublous times.

We notice that there is a separation between the "7 weeks" (**, and**) threescore and two weeks. This separation with a "comma" and the word "and" tells us that these are not part of the same period of time, but are added together, making it 7 weeks/years + threescore and two weeks. This period of *"threescore and two weeks" refers to a period of 3.5 years*. I know and understand that some will say, "How?" I will answer you shortly. Let's keep looking at what is happening during this portion of time. This time is the period where the rebuilding will actually take place, which as we know can only happen after the land has rested for 7 weeks/years. This rebuilding will go on for about 3.5 years. What happens after these 3.5 years?

> ***Daniel 9:26*** *(KJV)*
> **26** And **after** threescore and two weeks **shall Messiah** *be **cut off***, but not for himself:...

Proving to us that this period of rebuilding will not be during the first 7 week/years portion, but clearly taking place during the next 3.5 year portion of time. Once this time is over, **Messiah** would be **"cut off"**. This brings me to where I said I would answer your question about the 3.5 years.

We discussed Psalm 90:10 in chapter two, but we now need to consider it to understand Daniel's count.

> ***Psalm 90:10*** *(KJV)*
> **10** The days of our years are **threescore years and ten** (our 70 years we were looking at again); and if by reason *of strength* they be **fourscore years** (80 years), yet is their *strength* **labour** (H5999) **and sorrow** (H205) (; for it is **soon** ***cut off***, and we **fly away**.

Meaning from 70 to 80 years **is labour (H5999)** miserable (-sery), pain (-ful), perverseness, sorrow, toil, travail, trouble, wearisome, wickedness. **And Sorrow (H205)** trouble, vanity, wickedness; specifically an idol: - affliction, evil, false, idol, iniquity, mischief, mourners (-ing), naught, sorrow, unjust, unrighteous, vain, vanity, wicked (-ness.)

Then a short period of time called; **soon** (or about 6 months)

So we have from 70 to 80 + .5 years = 10.5 years to; **cut off**

So far we have had 7 years land at rest + 3.5 years rebuilding = 10.5 years to *Messiah,* **cut off** in Daniel 9.

To complete the picture of the evidence in **Psalm 90:10,** we next have; ***we fly away***. This period of time is the 3.5 years given us in **Revelation 12:14** that says she will "**fly away**" on eagles wings to a place protected for a time, and times, and half a time, or 3.5 years, which brings the completed picture of **Psalm 90:10** to 14 years.

And this is now where the rest of Daniel 9 gets very revealing and in greater detail. We just read that "Messiah" was cut off. This portion of time was not the first 7 years. This tells us that Messiah must be the one here during this next period of 3.5 years during the rebuilding, since **He is** the one being "cut off"! So after the 7 years of the land taking her rest, which is the 6 years of Seals judgments and the 7th year rest period, the next 3.5 years the Lord is here to watch over the rebuilding of Jerusalem before being "cut off".

So can we prove this is actually the Messiah and not just a reference of some anointed person? For one, we see Him coming at the end of the 6th seal.

> ***Revelation 6:16-17*** *(KJV)*
> **16** And said to the mountains and rocks, Fall on us, and **hide us from the face of him that sitteth on the throne, and from the wrath of the Lamb:**
> **17** For the great day of his wrath is come; and who shall be able to stand?

Also in:

> ***Revelation 14:1*** *(KJV)*
> **1** And I looked, and, lo, **a Lamb stood *on the mount Sion*,** and with him an hundred forty and four thousand, having his Father's name written in their foreheads.

He is coming at the end of the 6th seal or end of the first 6 of the 7 years. And next we read in Revelation 7 that the 144,000 are being sealed for their upcoming work during Trumpets. In Revelation 14 we see Him standing on **Mount Zion** with the 144,000. In the second half of Revelation 7 Mark's group has been raptured. Remember, the rebuilding cannot yet begin until the 7 years are completed. You may have asked yourself, "What is He doing standing on Mount Zion?" I will not go into all the details here, however you can make a mental note of it as you will see it mentioned in other parts of the books as well. Let me show you another place that connects this timing on Mount Zion to this period of Him being here when the rebuilding is to begin. It is truly incredible.

> ***Zechariah 8:3*** *(KJV)*
> **3** Thus saith the LORD; **I am returned** ***unto Zion***, and will dwell in the midst of Jerusalem: and Jerusalem shall be called a city of truth; *and **the Mountain** of the LORD of Hosts the holy mountain*.

A few verses later, in the same chapter, he goes on to tell us they will now begin to rebuild and that before this time there was no one to rebuild, because it was "affliction" time and everyone was "set against their neighbour", referring to the tribulation of Seals happening.

> ***Zechariah 8:9-10*** *(KJV)*
> **9** Thus saith the LORD of hosts; Let your hands be strong, ye that hear in these days these words by the mouth of the prophets, which were in the day that the foundation of the house of the LORD of

hosts was laid, *that the temple might be built*.
10 For before these days there was no hire for
man, nor any hire for beast; neither was there any
peace to him that went out or came in ***because of***
the affliction: for *I set all men every one against*
his neighbour.

These are clearly showing us the Lord will be here on Mount Zion at the time the rebuilding will begin after the first 7 years are completed. And in the chapter called "*The Books Have Opened!*", you will see this incredible connection as to why this is spoken of in Zechariah 8 of all chapters. But now, why or how could Messiah be "cut off"? Looking at what follows 10.5 years (7years + 3.5 years) in the 14 year revelation, we see that it puts us at mid-Trumpets time frame or at the first "Woe!" of the 5th trumpet, which is when satan will have been cast down, having lost his battle against Michael as we read in Revelation 12.

Revelation 12:7-9 *(KJV)*
7 And there was war in heaven: Michael and his
angels fought against the dragon; and the dragon
fought and his angels,
8 And prevailed not; neither was their place found
any more in heaven.
9 And the great dragon was cast out, that old
serpent, called the Devil, and Satan, which
deceiveth the whole world: he was cast out into the
earth, and his angels were cast out with him.

Which is then followed by telling us the time frame that this happens.

Revelation 12:12-15 *(KJV)*
12 Therefore rejoice, ye heavens, and ye that dwell
in them. **Woe** (this is the first Woe) to the inhabiters
of the earth and of the sea! for the devil is come
down unto you, having great wrath, because he
knoweth that he hath but a short time.
13 And when the dragon saw that he was cast unto
the earth, he persecuted the woman which brought
forth the man child.
14 And the woman was given two wings of a great
eagle, that she might fly into the wilderness, into
her place, where she is nourished for ***a time, and
times, and half a time***, from the face of the
serpent.
15 And the serpent cast out of his mouth **water as
a flood after the woman**, that he might cause her
to be carried away from the flood.

We see this is the same 3.5 year reference we showed for **Psalm 90:10** after the 10.5 years, the "**we fly away"**, which was also the reference to **Daniel 9:26's** 10.5 year point to the "cut off". This would tell us the reason for Messiah's "cut off", because satan has now been cast down to the earth.

So continuing with the rest of Daniel 9:

Daniel 9:26 *(KJV)*
26 ... and the people of the **p**rince that shall come **shall destroy the city and the sanctuary**; and the end thereof shall be **with a flood**, and unto **the end of the war** desolations are determined.

Now we can understand who this lower case "p" prince is. With Messiah "cut off" we can understand how it is that they will be able to destroy some of the city and sanctuary that has been rebuilt over the last 3.5 years. The next question is, "What is this "**with a flood**" telling us?"

After satan has been cast down to the earth, he will go after them with "**a flood**". However, we read in verse 16 that the Lord will open the earth and swallow the flood satan sends after them. As we continue in Daniel 9:26 we read, "unto **the end of the war**". Meaning there is a coming of an end to a war that started around the time satan was cast down to the earth and went after the women with a flood. It turns out we have that war revealed to us in Revelation 11.

> ***Revelation 11:7*** *(KJV)*
> **7** And when they shall have finished their testimony (the two witnesses), the beast that ascendeth out of the bottomless pit, shall **make war** against them, and ***shall*** *overcome them,* and kill them.

The beast ascending out of the bottomless pit is when satan will be cast down and the pit opened at the 5th trumpet, the first "Woe!".

Many think satan will kill the two witnesses right away after being cast down as they finish their 1260 days of testimony, which will happen during the first half of Trumpets while the rebuilding was taking place. If that were the case, why would scripture tell us he "makes **war** against them". It would have simply said, "he then kills them." We are told in the same chapter when they will be killed. This is only days before the end of the 6th trumpet time. This war will last for 2.5 years before they are killed.

Let me prove this 2.5 years more clearly. First, we have understood that to the point of the "cut off" of Messiah was 10.5 years of the total 14 years. Leaving us only 3.5 years to go. We then saw in Revelation 12:14 that the ones taken to safety will be taken to safety until the end of the 14 years, because it told us *time, and times, and half a time*, which was explained earlier, the "comma and the word "and" is a separation and addition. This is then 1 + 2 + 0.5 or 3.5 years to the end of the total of 14 years.

However, that last portion of Daniel 9:26 does not go to the very end of the story. We find the answer in Daniel 12 to how long it is.

> ***Daniel 12:6-7*** *(KJV)*
> **6** And one said to the man clothed in linen, which was upon the waters of the river, How long shall it be to the end of these wonders?
> **7** And I heard the man clothed in linen, which was upon the waters of the river, when he held up his right hand and his left hand unto heaven, and swear by him that liveth for ever that it shall be ***for a time, times, and an half***, and *when he shall have accomplished to scatter the power of the holy people, all these things shall **be finished***.

He is told this final portion will be for "a time, times, and an half". This is not the same as *time, **and** times, and half a time.* **The difference is one year**! This description of time does not have the "**and**" as an addition between "time, times", which means it is not adding the two, but simply counting 1, 2, then + 0.5 = 2.5 years, which gives us our answer as to how long satan brings chaos and will reign on earth for.

In Daniel 12:7 we read that at the end of that time "all these things shall **be finished**". The same as we read in Revelation 10.

> ***Revelation 10:7*** *(KJV)*
> **7** But in the days of the voice of the seventh angel, *when he **shall begin to sound***, the mystery of God should **be finished**, as he hath declared to his servants the prophets.

Up to this point in Daniel 9 to the end of verse 26, we have:

- 7 years land at rest (which is tribulation of Seals happening),
- 3.5 years city and the temple being rebuilt (until Messiah is "cut off"),
- 2.5 years Satan takes his reign (at the time of the first "Woe!" of the 5th trumpet,to the end of the 6th trumpet)
  = 13 years, leaving us **one year** to go and one verse!

> ***Daniel 9:27*** *(KJV)*
> **27** And **he** shall **confirm the covenant** with many for **one week**: and in the midst of the week **he** shall cause the sacrifice and the oblation **to cease**, and for the overspreading of abominations **he** shall

make it desolate, even **until the consummation**, and that determined shall be poured upon the desolate.

So now who is the "**he**" that will confirm the covenant? It is **Messiah Jesus** coming back feet down on the Mount of Olives after satan's 2.5 years when "all these things shall be finished". It was the Lord who made the covenant at the time of the end of Seals, which is the beginning of Trumpets. He then broke the covenant, because satan was cast down and the pit opened. As we read of this covenant in Zechariah 11.

Zechariah 11:10-11 *(KJV)*
10 And I took my staff, even Beauty, and cut it asunder, that I might ***break my covenant*** which **I had made with all the people**.
11 *And it was broken in that day*.

I will bring greater understanding in context as to why this is found in Zechariah 11 of all places, in the chapter, "*The Books have Opened!*".

So when He then returns feet down once and for all, **He** will "confirm". (H1396) exceed, confirm, be great, be mighty, prevail, put to more [strength], *strengthen*, *be stronger*, be valiant. He will thus confirm that covenant He broke when satan was cast down, which will be in that final "**1 week/year"**!

Look closely at the wording in verse 27. **He** is going to make the sacrifices end and because of the abominations, **He** is going to make it "desolate" (H8074) that is, devastate, make desolate (-ion, places), be destitute, destroy (self), (lay, lie, make) waste.

Many have taught that this "he" is satan, but why would satan, who was causing the "overspreading of abominations" and the "sacrifices" be the one that is going to destroy what he was actually doing? It is clear that the **HE** who is going to make desolate at the end, is not satan, but Jesus Messiah, putting an end to satan's reign and we read this again in Zechariah.

> ***Zechariah 14:4*** *(KJV)*
> **4** And his feet shall stand on that day upon the mount of Olives (not mount Zion this time final time), which is before Jerusalem on the east, and the mount of Olives shall cleave in the midst.

And a few verses later we read about this destruction He, Jesus, is going to bring against all those who came against Jerusalem.

> ***Zechariah 14:12*** *(KJV)*
> **12** And this shall be the plague wherewith **the LORD will smite all the people that have fought against Jerusalem**; Their flesh shall **consume** away while they stand upon their feet, and their eyes shall **consume** away in their holes, and their tongue shall **consume** away in their mouth.

Just as what we read next in Dan.9:27... even until **the consummation (H3617)**... **consummation** (H3617) a completion; adverbially completely; also destruction: - **altogether, (be, utterly) consume (-d)**, consummation (-ption),

For generations the Church has believed that Daniel 9:27's "one week" is about the antichrist. How or why could this thinking have been possible for so long?

The answer is that the books had been sealed until the time of the end as we were told in Daniel 12:4. The revelation of who the Gospels are speaking to was so vital to our understanding of rightly dividing the Word in truth. The revelation of the final two sets of 7, or as we say 14 years, was the key to opening the End Time books. Once this was understood, the books began to reveal themselves one after another and the End Time picture became more and more clear than it had ever been in all of history. Not because I did anything special, but because it was TIME!

In summary: Daniel 9:24-27 is giving us another clear image with greater detail of the 14 years.

- **7 years** starting with Jerusalem having been attacked, causing the land to enjoy her sabbath rest, which is during the time of Seals.

- **3.5 years** when Messiah having come down on Mount Zion is overseeing the rebuilding of Jerusalem during the first 3.5 years of Trumpets until "cut off" at the casting down of satan to the earth.

- **2.5 years,** which is the beginning of the first "Woe!" at the opening of the pit, which is at the 5th trumpet beginning the second half of

Trumpets, right up until the end of the 6th trumpet.

+

- **1** year, which is the 7th trumpet when Lord returns feet down on the Mount of Olives and destroys all who came against Jerusalem.

= 14 Years!

CHAPTER 5

THE DIFFERENCES AND THE TRUTH

In this chapter we will discuss the differences between the Pre, Mid, and Post tribulation beliefs. For those new to this wording, it means the difference between the belief in a group taken away in what is called the "rapture", either Pre (before the tribulation begins), Mid (of course, the halfway point) or Post (at the end). This is important that we unravel the mystery of the differences of opinions that have been around for hundreds of years that has been causing so much division in the Church. The reality is that there is plenty of scripture to support all three beliefs. I can speak for myself when I say before the books began to open, I bounced back and forth a few times between believing it was "Pre" compared to "Mid". The reason being that the scriptures that were being presented by those in their position of "Pre" and "Mid", were convincing to support their position. However, as the books began to open and I understood that the gospels were speaking to different groups in their End Time understanding and the 14 years began to reveal itself, I could clearly see the truth. Which is exactly what we are going to show you here in this chapter. THEY ARE ALL TRUE!

The only way to see and understand it, is with the understanding of who the gospels are speaking to and the 14 years. That is why the first two chapters of this book are so vital to understand the rest of the revealing of the opened books. Also the reason why I call those first two revelations, "The 2 Keys to End Time Understanding".

This is no light task to reveal, considering it is something that has been debated for hundreds of years. Innumerable books have been written on the topic, however, I am going to reveal it to you in a chapter. Not because it could not have it's own book, but because the keys to truly seeing and understanding it have already been given to you in the first two chapters. Once you see it, you will not be able to unsee the understanding, having the 2 keys as a foundation as to who the gospels are speaking to and the 14 years.

So let's first begin with why the church for generations has only believed the tribulation was only a single 7 year period and what are the different ways in which they teach it?

> ***Daniel 9:27*** *(KJV)*
> **27** And he shall confirm the covenant with many **for one week**: and in the midst of the week he shall cause the sacrifice and the oblation to cease, and for the overspreading of abominations he shall make it desolate, even until the consummation, and that determined shall be poured upon the desolate.

This one verse has been the main cause of all of the differences, on the surface. I will get to that, "on the surface", in a moment.

So why this one verse? Because what has been taught is that the "one week" means 7 years and the "midst of the week" is the midpoint of tribulation when the enemy will break the covenant that he will have made with many. The reason for this view of "one week" equaling 7 years, is because of one of the descriptions in the understanding of the word "week". This word means days in a week, and has been taught as meaning 7 days in a week, which must be 7 years. In this thinking, the teaching says the first portion of verses 24-26 have already been fulfilled when Jesus came the first time. Thus they no longer have anything to do with the End Times, only verse 27 to their understanding. This has been the teaching for the past several generations. However, if you have read our Daniel 9 chapter, you will have already understood with clarity that this thinking is completely inaccurate. It has brought even more confusion and unanswerable questions. Daniel 9 also revealed to us that "one week" in the End Times revelation is literally to be understood as "one year". Exactly as the 70 weeks, 7 weeks, etc. They are all to be understood as years.

Now as I mentioned, there is more to why they have this thinking. The "on the surface" part of it is their understanding of 7 years. Why they think 7 years only has a much deeper reason. I would say it is subconsciously. The reason for this "bend" towards 7 years is that all of it goes back to being taught from Matthew. You might be thinking, "What? What does the gospel of Matthew have to do with them only seeing 7 years for the tribulation?" Let me explain. You have just come to understand who the gospels are speaking to and that Luke is speaking to the Bride of Christ, Mark is to the sleeping church who will go through the Seals judgment, and Matthew is to the Jews/Judah during the Trumpet judgments. You have also understood that the tribulation of Seals and Trumpets is two sets of 7 years.

What has caused them to see or understand only 7 years in the first place, is the fact that the entire church has been teaching eschatology from a foundation in MATTHEW. They base it from Matthew's discourse in chapter 24. Meaning their perspective and the perspective they have been teaching everyone from, is that of the Jews/Judah. And what portion of time during the tribulation is to Matthew's group? The last 7 years of Trumpets.

Most of the church at this point, with the exception of those who have come to understand these revelations, believe that there will only be a 7 year tribulation. There are two ways that their pre-tribulation teaching will play out. The general belief is that it is going to be 3.5 years of Seals and 3.5 years of Trumpets. And within this thinking there are those who are Pre, Mid and Post and each believes that at their point the rapture will happen.

Now there is something else that they have missed in their teachings as well. According to GOD's law, it is always 6 and the 7th is rest, as we discussed in "*When the Years Just Don't' Add Up*".

> ***Leviticus 23:3*** *(KJV)*
> **3** Six days shall work be done: but the seventh day is the sabbath of rest, an holy convocation.

Leviticus 25:3-4 *(KJV)*

3 Six years thou shalt sow thy field, and six years thou shalt prune thy vineyard, and gather in the fruit thereof;

4 But in the seventh year shall be a sabbath of rest unto the land, a sabbath for the LORD: thou shalt neither sow thy field, nor prune thy vineyard.

It applies to days of a week, as well as to a 7 year cycle in which the 7th year is called the Shmita year of "release" for the land and debts. Right off the bat there is an issue in saying the tribulation is going to be 7 years.

Let me share what to me is the most telling and revealing of how this Matthew foundation has caused all of the first 7 year portion of Mark to have been missed, in this first view of their Pre-tribulation "rapture". In this thinking they teach that the whole church is going to be going in the Pre "rapture". Anyone who has simply said, "I believe in Jesus", gets to go. What a shock and devastation they are in for! Because you see, with a Matthew perspective and believing you go before Matthew's tribulation begins, it would mean you are at the end of Mark's time. And the end of Mark's portion is the end of Seals! Just as we read here about the great multitude now standing before the Lord AFTER the Seals judgments.

Revelation 7:9-10 *(KJV)*

9 After this I beheld, and, **lo, a great multitude, which no man could number, of all nations**, and kindreds, and people, and tongues, ***stood before***

the throne, and before the Lamb, clothed with white robes, and palms in their hands;
10 And cried with a loud voice, saying, Salvation to our God which sitteth upon the throne, and unto the Lamb.

This great multitude, which no man can number before the throne, is the "rapture" of the whole church. The issue though is that it is not Pre, it is Mid! Are you seeing how this Matthew foundation has completely confused all End Time teachings? They are teaching a Pre because they can see it in scripture, but they are teaching it from a Mid perspective. In reality, what they say follows the Pre, is in fact Mid. This is when the antichrist will show up and settle the confusion and devastation due to a billion and a half people having vanished off the earth. Bringing about a peace deal that will then allow Israel to rebuild their third temple. At the middle point of their 7 years, the antichrist is going to break that peace deal he made and step into the temple and declare himself to be God, which is the Matthew 24 "abomination of desolation" that will take place. Then the Trumpets judgment will begin and go to the end of the 7 years, which they see as the next half of the 7 years, being 3.5 years to go.

Depending how far along you are into this book, you will realize that they are confused and are actually seeing the 7 years of Trumpets. What do we know happens at the end of the first 7 years of Seals? The Lord has come down on Mount Zion, the "was caught up" rapture takes place, and it is the Lord Himself who will make the covenant with all people. He will allow the rebuilding of destroyed

Jerusalem and the temple to begin, NOT the antichrist. The antichrist's portion of time will have come to an end at the end of the 6th seal as we have shown. What happens at the middle of Trumpets is not the antichrist breaking the covenant, but Christ breaking the covenant He made with all people. He is breaking it, because this is the point when satan is cast down and will open the pit, etc. So we can see how they are seeing part of it, but unfortunately completely mixing it up with portions that had already happened during the Seals judgment. So their Pre teaching view is that everyone goes. However, it is going to be a devastating shock to the 90% of the church who will end up remaining through to the end of Seals. Those who have been taught this view and had not readied themselves for the Lord, thinking all they needed was to believe in Him and they would get to go before it all begins, will be confounded and very livid with the church and pastors. They will be overwhelmed with absolute confusion and devastation.

And by the way, this view as well as the others in this 7 year only belief, tell us that the antichrist and satan are the same. Make no mistake, they are of the same spirit and satan gives him his power and authority, but this does not make them the same. Otherwise scripture would not have told us this the following.

> ***Revelation 16:13*** *(KJV)*
> **13** And I saw **three** unclean spirits like frogs come out of the mouth **of the dragon**, and out of the mouth **of the beast**, and out of the mouth **of the false prophet**.

How could there be seen **three** come out, from the beast (antichrist), false prophet and dragon (satan)? This is because the antichrist and satan are two. But the reason these groups tell us they are one, is because again, they cannot see that they have missed half the tribulation, and cannot account as to where the other would be if they were separate.

Now here is another view that believes the same 7 years as 3.5 years for Seals and 3.5 years for Trumpets. However, where they differ is they believe the "rapture" is Mid and they see it as being at the end of Seals, which is good in the sense of the actual rapture of the whole church. Yet not a good thing when you realize they are telling everyone it will be about 3.5 years into the tribulation that they could expect to be raptured. And the reason this is not good either, is because as they are telling everyone the rapture is coming and that the Lord is about to get them at this time, the one who is actually showing up around about this time of the middle of Seals judgment is the antichrist, around the point of getting his power to continue 42 months. Now you might say, "Why would they still be thinking the rapture is still coming in 3.5 years?" The answer is, very few will believe that the group taken at the beginning, the Luke group, was the Pre-tribulation rapture. They will say the number of people who vanished was too few to have been the rapture and many of them will say..."because I am still here".

Are you seeing how devastating this Matthew foundation is to those who will still be here to the end? They are not seeing and understanding that the scriptures of Revelation 7 are clearly telling us the RAPTURE of the church is going to happen at the end of Seals. They have properly seen the rapture as Mid, although very importantly, in the wrong year count. However, they have not understood that the Pre is not the rapture as it has come to have been understood, what we know as the ESCAPE.

What they have done is point to everything that is fairly easy to understand as proving the rapture in Mid. Like Revelation 12:5's "was caught up", which is clearly after devastation has already begun in the first few verses, and in Revelation 7 seeing it after the Seals judgments. What they have missed is the portion that has told us "**before**" it all begins, or "**before she travails**", she brings forth. There is a group that is being taken out Pre that is not the "rapture" and many have come to understand this from the famous verse people like to point to as Pre, and are correct in doing so.

> ***Isaiah 66:7*** *(KJV)*
> **7** ***Before she travailed**, **she brought forth***, before her pain came, she was delivered of a man child.

Meaning before the tribulation or we would say Pre-tribulation. If we go to Revelation 12 we can see where this Pre must happen before her travail has begun.

> ***Revelation 12:1-2*** *(KJV)*
> **1** And there appeared a great wonder in heaven; a woman clothed with the sun, and the moon under her feet, and upon her head a crown of twelve stars:

2 And she being with child *cried*, **travailing in birth**, and **pained** to be delivered.

I love it when scripture is so clear in what it is telling us. This was the beginning as I mentioned, when the books began to open to me. The realization that the first group must go **before** verse 2 of Revelation 12, and not as we were being taught as being the one from verse 5.

Revelation 12:3-5 *(KJV)*
3 And there appeared another wonder in heaven; and behold a great red dragon, having seven heads and ten horns, and seven crowns upon his heads.
4 And his tail drew the third part of the stars of heaven, and did cast them to the earth: and the dragon stood before the woman which was ready to be delivered, for to devour her child as soon as it was born.
5 And she brought forth a man child, who was to rule all nations with a rod of iron: and her child **was caught up** unto God, and to his throne.

This is clearly after much devastation has taken place, mentioning her travailing in pain of verse 2 and a third of the stars being cast down to the earth in verse 4. Proving that this "was caught up" is the rapture they all speak about, yet it is at the end of Seals. So where else can we understand this other Pre that is not the rapture, but is **like** a rapture? We have covered it in the chapter revealing the 14 years. But I love sharing this one so let me remind you of it.

2 Corinthians 12:2-4 *(KJV)*
2 I knew a man in Christ *above* ***fourteen years***

ago, (whether in the body, I cannot tell; or whether
out of the body, I cannot tell: God knoweth;) ***such
an one*** (the wording means "like", "similar") ***caught
up*** (rapture) **to the third heaven**. (***Pre***)
3 And I knew such a man, (whether in the body, or
out of the body, I cannot tell: God knoweth;)
4 How that he ***was caught up*** (here you find the
same wording from Revelation 12:5 - **into
paradise**, (**Mid**) and heard unspeakable words,
which it is not lawful for a man to utter.

Here is another view, however, I do not need to spend much time on it except to tell you how they count it. They see the 7 years of Seals and Trumpets as overlapping each other. People have come up with all sorts of ways to try and make sense of it all in a 7 year period. And within this group you still have the same Pre, Mid and Post thinking and the Pre in the similar sense of the whole church going at the start.

There are many out there who believe in Pre, but how they understand it will play out is where all the confusion begins. They are aware of scripture clearly telling them not all will go first, yet they are also seeing scripture that tells them the rapture is after some tribulation, as we read in Revelation 12:1-5. And then they try to understand what they are seeing in the paradigm of only 7 years with their foundation, unbeknownst to them, still stuck in Matthew. And we wonder why the confusion and so many struggling to see what we are sharing. This was and is the reason the first revelations that need to be understood are who the Gospels are speaking to and then the 14 years, the 2 keys to End Time understanding.

As for those in the Post tribulation thinking, they too have a piece that is correct, yet in complete misunderstanding of it. They believe it will be at the end of 7 years, their view of the end of the tribulation. They do not believe that there is any Pre or Mid that will happen, but that it will only be when the Lord returns. And in their thinking they would tell you that it is when the Lord will return at the end of Seals and Trumpets, feet down on the Mount of Olives, all in 7 years. Yet as we have come to realize, the end of that timeframe of 7 years will not be when the Lord will return feet down on the Mount of Olives, but at the end of Seals when He will return on Mount Zion, that mountain carved without hands. When the actual rapture of the whole church will take place, not after Trumpets, but after Seals. So in their post tribulation beliefs of when, being after 7 years, which they think is the end of it all, they are actually incorrect in their understanding, because their view is unbeknownst to them, about the timeframe of the rapture of the church. Again, even in this line of thinking, the issue goes back to their foundation being in the understanding from Matthew.

So in summary of these groups:

- The "Pre" has the understanding of the Escape "like a rapture" and not the rapture, that is to say the difference as discussed in **2 Corinthians 12:2-4,** but are confusing it with the time when the whole remaining church will be taken, which is in reality at the end of Seals judgment.
- The "Mid" are seeing it as the rapture in the right place as the church as a whole, except they

missed seeing the Escape of the Pre, and they believe it is going to be after only 3.5 years into the tribulation to reach the end of Seals. Unfortunately this will only be about half way through, during the antichrist timeframe, and not yet the end of the Seals judgment.

- And the "Post" of course miss the Escape, but are seeing the rapture, in the right year timeframe, however, when that time actually is and what they are expecting, will not yet be the end of it all, but only the end of Seals.

And finally, let me end with this viewpoint that is also out there. Now if the Lord has not revealed the opened books, I believe this would have been the category I would have been a part of. This group believes in Pre, but they believe we are at the end of the Seals judgments and right now waiting for the 6th seal to happen. Then the Lord will come and seal those 144,000 and rapture the whole church. After that it will be the 7 years of tribulation, but that it will be all Trumpets. This actually would make the most sense in a 7 year thinking when believing the whole church gets raptured Pre, and that what follows is only for Judah or what is known as "Jacob's Trouble". The only issue is, they have skipped the seals judgment as being part of the tribulation time and chalked them up to events that have happened on earth over the past 2000 years since Christ resurrection. Apparent good thinking when your foundation is in Matthew. Except there is a big problem that still puts them at the end of Mark's gospel timeframe that they have missed, including Seals. They had to explain the

Seals somehow? Why? Because like all the other views they are still stuck in 7 years and a foundation set in Matthew.

The answer is given to us in 2 Corinthians 12.

- **Pre**; Luke's group, **<u>Escape</u>** of the Bride, "Like" a rapture, to the 3rd Heaven, "Above/ Before" the 14 years begin.
- **Mid**; Mark's group, the **<u>Rapture</u>** of the Church, to Paradise, After the Seals judgments, in the 7th year.
- **Post**; Matthew's group, Jew's/Judah, no one being taken, **<u>Return</u>** of the Lord feet down on the Mount of Olives, After the 6 years of Trumpets judgments, and 13 total years are complete. He will fulfill the 14th year in the judgment of all who came against Jerusalem.

Originally I was not going to add this chapter to the book, because of a very tight timeframe to get the book done. I did not think we would get the chance. But I am happy I was able to with the help of the Holy Spirit's leading, and the help I have received from those involved in the producing this book. I believe it is a very important chapter to help bring about the understanding as to why there has been these differences. How was this all so misunderstood for so long? The answer brothers and sisters is that it simply was not yet the time for the books to have opened. GOD's plan will be completed perfectly according to His word, but the decision as to whether you will be in the

Pre or Mid group is still up to you...until the Pre has been removed.

This is great news for all who have been praying for family and friends who have not yet given their lives to Christ as their Lord and Savior. They WILL still have a chance to go to Paradise in the rapture. So do not stop praying for them and be sure to leave this book for them to find and send to others while you still can.

CHAPTER 6

THE END TIME 7 CHURCHES

This is an awesome revelation, one that has also been a mystery for a long time. As I have been writing and considering just the number of revelations that have been written in this book, I am almost brought to tears again. This one, at the time of writing, is still pretty fresh and only came to be understood a few months ago. I had begun to understand a couple of the churches written in Revelations in their portion of the End Times. Like everyone else, it just was not clear to be able to say that we fully get it. Until I came across a similar chart to the one below while online doing a search on the "Church Ages". Within minutes of reading this they all clicked and made sense in their End Time timeframe. What was interesting, is the site where I found it was using it to show church historian's beliefs that can be seen in the 7 churches during the church age that is playing out. They themselves did not believe it was the case and simply wanted to show the other side's view by sharing the chart. I am grateful they did, because now I can show you that the understanding of the type and shadow that is played out over the 2000 years of church history is indeed correct. I will also further prove what is coming in their End Time revealing as scriptures tell us.

Ecclesiastes 1:9 *(KJV)*
9 The thing that <u>hath been</u>, it is that which <u>shall be</u>;

> and that <u>which is done</u> is that which <u>shall be done</u>: and there is **no new thing under the sun**.

This is an important scripture as the truth of it is seen in what we have discussed in this book with regard to the future, specifically the End Times. This will also apply to the 7 churches. To bring it into even greater clarity, I would say it more like this: "was", "is", and "is to come". Now at first that would not appear to make much sense, because there was no church in the "<u>was</u>", or before Christ. Church did not begin until the "<u>is</u>" that we would be considered in the tail end of right now, which started at Pentecost. You may have heard pastors talk about this in the past. They would say we are in the Laodicea church age now, the last one. Saying that this is why there has been so much falling away that has taken place over the past few decades. And they were right in what they were saying. So what do these two first portions mean? If you go to the chart below in the column named, "Israel's History Typified", you will see that these are the events before Christ in Israel's history that had their significance in the "was" that tied into the "is" of current church history since Christ. What church historians and theologians discovered is that there was an association between the two over similar periods of time on both sides of Christ.

SEVEN STAGES OF CHURCH HISTORY

Church	Church History Typified	Dates (AD)	Israel's History Typified	Verses
Ephesus	The Apostolic Church	30-100	The Day of Israel's Espousals (Exodus)	Rev 2: 1-7
Smyrna	The Church of the Roman Persecution	100-313	The Period of Israel's Wanderings (Numbers)	Rev 2: 5-11
Pergamum	The Church of the Age of Constantine	313-600	The Wilderness Period (Numbers)	Rev 2: 12-17
Thyatira	The Church of the Dark Ages	600-1517	The Wilderness Period (Numbers)	Rev 2: 18-29
Sardis	The Church of the Reformation	1517-1648	The Period of Israel's Kings (1 and 2 Kings)	Rev 3: 1-6
Philadelphia	The Church of the Great Missionary Movement	1648-1900	The Period of Israel's Removal (1 and 2 Chronicles)	Rev 3: 7-13
Laodicea	The Church of the Apostasy	1900-present day	The Period of Judah's Kings (2 Chronicles)	Rev 3: 14-22

So for example, the first church, Ephesus, in the "was" of the history of Israel that they associated it with, was the Day of Israel's Espousals or the Exodus. And in the "is" it was the Apostolic age after Christ was taken to heaven. The corresponding years in the "is" are from AD 30 to 100 approximately. People like to debate the years, but that has nothing to do with what we are revealing here. The "approximate" years are fine and will prove the revelation regardless. The point is the reference of all of them in their period of time that is just astounding. It is not difficult to see, but I will share another to make the point.

Let's look at Sardis. The "was" they associated with the Period of Israel's Kings, and in the "is" of church history, it was the time of the Reformation in the years corresponding to AD 1577 to 1648. And why these events for each were associated with these years, was based on the wording given to us in the 7 churches of Revelation 2 and 3 to what was happening in those times. This is precisely how we are going to do it in the "is to come". I am sure you have gotten the picture by now that, without the keys, this too could never have been understood. Unlike the "is" of the past, almost 2000 years, they had to be looked at in hindsight to understand where we are. But it was an incredible understanding. So much so, that if those before had not discovered it, I could not have stood on their shoulders to see this "is to come" revelation.

So now let me show you this "<u>is to come</u>" for all 7 churches. Be sure to keep the 14 years in your thoughts and where Messiah was shown to be "cut off" at the middle of Trumpets, or 10.5 years into Seals and Trumpets judgment. At this point, one of the first questions people ask is, "What about the Luke group that escapes everything before the tribulation?" They have been taken already, as this is the beginning that represents the start of the tribulation of 14 years. They were the "overcomers" from among all these churches accounted worthy to escape all these things. These are the remaining who were not ready.

Another question people ask is when the time represented for one church, in its portion, is passed. Does that mean that the church that it represented is gone? The answer is no. The type and shadow is simply their representation in the time period they are found. Kind of like what we spoke about with the Seals. Each will have its time that it will represent, while another may also be happening at the same time, but have its greater effect during its appointed time. The 7 churches are all still here in one way or another in the "is", yet as of this writing we are considered to be in the last one, Laodicea. So it does not mean that they are no longer around.

THE CHURCH OF EPHESUS

> ***Revelation 2:1-2, 7*** *(KJV)*
> **1** Unto the angel of <u>*the church of Ephesus*</u> write; These things saith he that holdeth the seven stars in his right hand, who walketh in the midst of the seven golden candlesticks;
> **2** I know thy works, and thy labour, and thy patience, and how thou canst not bear them which are evil: and <u>thou hast tried them which say they</u>

are **apostles**, and are not, and hast found them liars:
7 He that hath an ear, let him hear what the Spirit saith unto the churches; To him that overcometh will I give to eat of the tree of life, which is in the midst of the paradise of God.

We can see Ephesus has a relation to Apostles and is the clue to the timing of the first End Time church period. In the end, this first period as revealed earlier in the book, is going to be a period many call the coming greatest Apostolic revival in all human history. It is going to begin after the Son of Man has left and the Holy Ghost will have come at what I earlier referred to as "Acts 2.0". This IS that period represented here as the Apostolic church. It is this group chosen by the Lord while here, to bring this revival about. And when the Lord comes on Mount Zion at the end of the 6th Seal, this group will go where the rapture group will be taken, which is paradise. The fact that they will be here until the end of Seals, shows us that their work will not simply end after this church age ends, but will continue to the rapture to Paradise. As in history with the Exodus, this represents the Escape having happened right as this time is about to begin.

THE CHURCH OF SMYRNA

Revelation 2:8-11 *(KJV)*
8 And unto the angel of *the church in Smyrna* write; These things saith the first and the last, which was dead, and is alive;
9 I know thy works, and tribulation, and poverty, (but thou art rich) and I know the blasphemy of

> them which say they are Jews, and are not, but are the synagogue of Satan.
> **10** Fear none of those things which thou shalt suffer: behold, the devil shall cast **some of you** into prison, that ye may be tried; and ye shall have tribulation ten days: be thou faithful **unto death**, and I will give thee a crown of life.
> **11** He that hath an ear, let him hear what the Spirit saith unto the churches; He that overcometh **shall not be hurt of the second death**.

Smyrna is loaded with information, but we are not going to go into each part. They are not told to "repent". Out of all the 7 churches, only they and Philadelphia are told not to repent. This is because those in Smyrna are those that will die for their faith during the tribulation. You see the connection to church history as persecution having begun, and in Israel's history we see this is the time of the wanderings. This persecution is what we would call the early stages of persecution, however the persecution coming against them will not stop. It will only get worse as we understand where we are in the tribulation. At this point we are in the first 2.5 years of Seals and there will be persecution unto death during the greatest revival. We can also understand that these are those who as persecution becomes worse, are found under the altar in Revelation 6:9 at the 5th seal. We see at the 5th seal they appear to have been there for a little while as they are crying out for GOD to avenge them. This group in Smyrna is then told they would not be hurt by the second death. What does that mean? The answer is found in

Revelation 20:4-6 *(KJV)*
4 And I saw thrones, and they sat upon them, and
judgment was given unto them: and I saw the souls
of them that were beheaded for the witness of
Jesus, and for the word of God, and which had not
worshipped the beast, neither his image, neither
had received his mark upon their foreheads, or in
their hands; **and they lived and reigned with
Christ a thousand years**.
5 But the rest of the dead lived not again until the
thousand years were finished. **This is the first
resurrection.**
6 Blessed and holy is he that hath part in the first
resurrection: **on such the second death hath no
power**, but they shall be priests of God and of
Christ, and shall reign with him a thousand years.

The ones from under the altar who died or you could say, put their necks on the line, for their faith in Christ. They are going to be resurrected at His return feet down and the second death will not hurt them after their 1000 years with the Lord. Wow! What an honor this group will be given!

THE CHURCH OF PERGAMUM

Revelation 2:12-14, 16-17 *(KJV)*
12 And to the angel of *the church in Pergamos*
write; These things saith he which hath the sharp
sword with two edges;
13 I know thy works, and where thou dwellest,
even where Satan's seat is: and thou holdest fast
my name, and hast not denied my faith, even in

those days wherein Antipas was my faithful martyr,
who was slain among you, where Satan dwelleth.
14 But I have a few things against thee, because
thou hast there them that hold the doctrine of
Balaam, who taught Balac to cast a stumblingblock
before the children of Israel, to eat things sacrificed
unto idols, and to commit fornication.
16 Repent; or else I will come unto thee quickly,
and will fight against them with the sword of my
mouth.
17 He that hath an ear, let him hear what the Spirit
saith unto the churches; To him that overcometh
will I give to eat of the hidden manna, and will
give him a white stone, and in the stone a new
name written, which no man knoweth saving he
that receiveth it.

In this scripture it tells us where satan's seat is and dwells, as the type of antichrist in his place. Then there is a doctrine of Balaam or a false belief being taught, which of course will be of the antichrist as the savior. If we go to church history we see it was the time of Constantine coming to power and he was a type of antichrist as well. When we look at Israel's history, we see this equals the time of the "wilderness". Well how fitting is that! This IS the period at which the antichrist will be given his power to continue 42 months. The exact same period of time found in Mark 13's discourse where we explained his "abomination of desolation" would begin at the time of his being given the power to continue 42 months, and the time of the mark of the beast coming. Christians will be hunted and also the reason why they will now at this point no longer try to understand, but will now be fleeing into the wilderness as Mark 13 told us at this time. When we look at the last verse for this church, we see the Lord told them He would give them of the "hidden manna" and it just so happens this is the group represented in its time as being the ones hiding in the wilderness. They will need to rely on the Lord's provision of manna while there. Next is the last church in chapter 2 and there is a good reason for that too. GOD is great! As I was about to add what this church tells us, I had to laugh at just how telling and awesome all this revealing is.

THE CHURCH OF THYATIRA

> ***Revelation 2:18, 22, 25-28*** *(KJV)*
> **18** And unto the angel of the *church in Thyatira*
> write; These things saith the Son of God, who hath
> his eyes like unto a flame of fire, and his feet are
> like fine brass;
> **22** Behold, I will cast her into a bed, and them that
> commit adultery with her *into* ***great tribulation***,
> except they repent of their deeds.
> **25** But that which ye have already hold fast ***till I***
> ***come***.
> **26** And he that overcometh, and keepeth my works
> unto **the end**, to him will I give power over the
> nations:
> **27** And he shall rule them **with a rod of iron**; as
> the vessels of a potter shall they be broken to
> shivers: even as I received of my Father.
> **28** And I will give him **the morning star**.

Going back to the chart, we see that church history tells us it was the Dark Ages and what do you think will relate to this time in the second half of Seals? The period during which the antichrist is ruling. Looking at Israel's history it tells us that it is still a time of being in the wilderness. Exactly what this period will still be until the end of the 6th seal. Can you see why He now says those who do not repent at this point will be going into the "great tribulation", which would mean the Trumpets judgments that will follow. Then we read "till I come" and "unto the end". That is because this will bring it to the End of the Seals judgment, which means the end of the 6th seal/year when He comes. We are also given the words "with a rod of iron" and "the morning star". Where do we read about this rod of iron?

> ***Revelation 12:5*** *(KJV)*
> **5** And <u>she brought forth a man child, who was to **rule all nations *with a rod of iron***</u>: and <u>her child **was caught up** unto God, and to his throne</u>.

And what time have we understood this to represent? The end of the 6th Seals as the Lord, the Morning Star, will have come on Mount Zion and will rule with the rod of iron, which is followed by the rapture as those "caught up" in the 7th year. It becomes so incredibly clear. And finally, let's not forget, I mentioned there was a reason why chapter 2 ended with this church. Are you seeing it now? It is because it is the end of the Seals judgment, after the 6th seal/years and the coming of the Lord on Mount Zion. So now with the Lord having come on Mount Zion, what have we come to understand comes next? The final 7th year of Seals.

THE CHURCH OF SARDIS.

Revelation 3:1, 3-5 *(KJV)*
1 And unto the angel of *the church in Sardis* write;
These things saith he that hath the seven Spirits of
God, and the seven stars; I know thy works, that
thou hast a name that thou livest, and art dead.
3 Remember therefore how thou hast received and
heard, and hold fast, and repent. If therefore thou
shalt not watch, I will come on thee as a thief, and
**thou shalt not know what hour I will come upon
thee**.
4 Thou hast a few names even in Sardis which have
not defiled their garments; and **they shall walk
with me in white**: for they are worthy.
5 He that overcometh, **the same shall be clothed
in white raiment**; and I will not blot out his name
out of the book of life, but I will confess his name
before my Father, and before his angels.

Here we see that church history tells us it is related to the time of the Reformation. The period in which the Bible began to get translated into English, the main language people understood instead of what Rome was reading, Latin, that fewer and fewer understood, and simply had to accept what was being said. This is also when the Bible started to come into the hands of the people and not just the clergy. Greater truths from the scriptures came to light.

It was also when Martin Luther in 1517 wrote his 95 Theses, denouncing much of what the Catholic Church had been doing and posted the Theses on the door of the Castle Church in Wittenberg, marking the start of the Protestant Reformation. Do you realize how this period of church history proves out in the "is to come" to have been so very important? To the point that in the description of this church is what brings us to the end of the true Church Age, that equals the year of the rapture in the 7th year of Seals! Consider what it is telling us in Israel's history. It is saying that it is the period of Israel's King(s). Do you get it? The Lord is here on Mount Zion and will be Israel's King. This is what we see in Daniel 7 that we have spoken about in a previous chapter.

> ***Daniel 7:13-14*** *(KJV)*
> **13** I saw in the night visions, and, behold, one like
> the **Son of man came** with the clouds of heaven,
> and came to the Ancient of days, and they brought
> him near before him.
> **14** And ***there was given him dominion***, and
> ***glory***, and ***a kingdom***, that all people, nations, and
> languages, should serve him: his dominion is an
> everlasting dominion, which shall not pass away,
> and his kingdom that which shall not be destroyed.

And according to the wording of this church we see those who were watching would be ready when He would come suddenly as that thief in the night, but those not watching would not be. Remember this is coming to the end of Mark's group time. And the two very last verses in Mark's discourse tell us:

> ***Mark 13:36-37*** *(KJV)*
> **36** Lest **coming suddenly** he find **you sleeping**.
> **37** And what I say unto you I say unto all, ***Watch***.

We also read within this church that they will be those who will walk with Him in white. This is exactly what we read will happen as we read in the scriptures regarding the first half of the 7th year of Seals, when this will happen.

Revelation 7:9-10 *(KJV)*
9 After this I beheld, and, lo, a great multitude,
which no man could number, of all nations, and
kindreds, and people, and tongues, stood before
the throne, and before the Lamb, ***clothed with***
white robes*, and palms in their hands*;
10 And cried with a loud voice, saying, Salvation to
our God which sitteth upon the throne, and unto
the Lamb.

THE CHURCH OF PHILADELPHIA

Revelation 3:7,9-10,12 *(KJV)*
7 And to the angel of the church in Philadelphia
write; These things saith he that is holy, he that is
true, he that hath the key of David, he that openeth,
and no man shutteth; and shutteth, and no man
openeth;
9 Behold, I will make them of the synagogue of
Satan, which say they are Jews, and are not, but do
lie; behold, I will make them to come and worship
before thy feet, and to know that I have loved thee.
10 Because thou hast kept the word of my
patience, *I also will* ***keep(G5083)*** *thee from the*
hour of temptation, which shall come upon all the
world, to try them that dwell upon the earth.
12 Him that overcometh will I make a pillar in the

> temple of my God, and he shall go no more out: and **I will write upon him the name of my God**, and the name of the city of my God, which is new Jerusalem, which cometh down out of heaven from my God: and I will write upon him my new name.

Many have thought this church was to the Gentile Bride of Christ. One of the reasons for that was that He would "keep" them from the hour of temptation, but that word does not mean He would remove them from it.

Keep **(G5083)** (a watch; perhaps akin to G2334); **to guard** (from loss or injury, properly by **keeping the eye upon**;

He will be watching over them protecting them from loss and NOT be taking them out of it.

And clearly in the writing of the name of GOD on them, we can most certainly understand this as being those 144,000 who were sealed having the Father's name written in their foreheads, as we also read in Revelation 14:1.

And if we follow the flow, the Seals and the first 7 years have now come to an end. Bringing us to the beginning of Trumpets and the Lord on Mount Zion as Israel's King, sending out the 144,000 who are going to be the "evangelists" during the first half of Trumpets. Just as we read was the period that followed in church history as the great missionary movement. They are the ones we spoke about in Luke 10 who Jesus sent out and when they returned to Him they were so excited by what they had been able to do in His name. Before He left them, if you recall, He said I beheld satan fall like lightning, and gave them greater power to tread serpents and scorpions, etc. This represents the middle of Trumpets when satan is cast to the earth. At the end of this period when Messiah is going to be cut off, the city, walls, and temple will have been rebuilt. It will also be the time when Messiah will break the covenant in one day, which He had made with all people, because satan is cast down. When we look at Israel's history for this church period, we see it is referred to as Israel's Removal. I call this crystal clear revelation. And this brings us to the final of the 7 churches of the End Times.

THE CHURCH OF LAODICEA

The revelation of this church in the end will not disappoint in what it reveals to us either.

> ***Revelation 3:14-16,20-21*** *(KJV)*
> **14** And unto the angel of the church of the
> Laodiceans write; These things saith the Amen, the faithful and true witness, the beginning of the creation of God;
> **15** I know thy works, that thou art neither cold nor
> hot: I would thou wert cold or hot.
> **16** So then because thou art lukewarm, and neither cold nor hot, **I will spue thee out of my mouth**.
> **20** Behold, ***I stand at the door***, and knock: if any man hear my voice, and open the door, I will come in to him, *and will sup with him, and he with me*.
> **21** To him that overcometh **will I grant to sit with me in my throne**, even as I also overcame, and am set down with my Father in his throne.

First let us take account of where we are at. Of course having been at the point where Messiah was being cut off, that put us at the middle of Trumpets or 3.5 years into Trumpets, or 10.5 years total. So with this in mind, let's see what church history has to tell us. It says that this church period represents the "apostasy church". Well let us have a look at what the scriptures tell us about the time of apostasy.

> ***2 Thessalonians 2:3-4*** *(KJV)*
> **3** Let no man deceive you by any means: for that day shall not come, except there come a **falling away(G646)** first, and that man of sin be revealed, **the son of perdition**;
> **4** Who opposeth and exalteth himself above all that is called God, or that is worshipped; *so that he as God sitteth in the temple of God*, **shewing himself that he is God.**

Falling away **(G646)** defection from truth (properly the state), ("**apostasy**"): - falling away, forsake.

The meaning of "falling away" means "apostasy". Look at "who" this time is connected to. It will be the time when the son of perdition is revealed and when He will sit "in the temple", which means it was rebuilt. Exactly when he will declare himself to be God. We know when the temple was finished, so that timing is correct. But how about the "son of perdition"? When do we know his time is? You will remember we covered this as well when I shared he "was", then "is not" and "shall be" when the pit is opened.

Revelation 17:8 *(KJV)*
8 The beast that thou sawest **was**, and **is not**; and **shall ascend out of the bottomless pit**, and ***go into perdition***: and they that dwell on the earth shall wonder, whose names were not written in the book of life from the foundation of the world, when they behold the beast that was, and is not, and yet is.

Once again proving this same period of time is the middle of Trumpets when satan has been cast down and the pit is opened, the time of the Apostasy or Great Falling Away. Concerning Israel's history, it tells us it was the period of Judah's King(s) and this "apostasy" who will be sitting in the temple claiming to be God? Satan. So this period of Judah's "king(s)" or in this reference as one of them is satan. Jesus is the one who told us.

John 8:39-44 *(KJV)*
39 They answered and said unto him, Abraham is our father. Jesus saith unto them, If ye were Abraham's children, ye would do the works of Abraham.
40 **But now ye seek to kill me**, a man that hath told you the truth, which I have heard of God: this did not Abraham.
41 **Ye do the deeds of your father**. Then said they to him, We be not born of fornication; we have one Father, even God.
42 Jesus said unto them, If God were your Father, ye would love me: for I proceeded forth and came from God; neither came I of myself, but he sent me.

43 Why do ye not understand my speech? even because ye cannot hear my word.
44 ***Ye are of your father the devil***, and the lusts of your father ye will do. He was a murderer from the beginning, and abode not in the truth, because there is no truth in him. When he speaketh a lie, he speaketh of his own: for he is a liar, and the father of it.

And the devil, the father of lies is the exact one here during this period. Looking at the wording for this church, we read that GOD is standing at the door about to come. The reason is that once this portion of satan's reign ends after 2.5 years, it will be the end of this church's portion. The Lord will return feet down on the Mount of Olives, having been at the door ready to return.

And finally, He says to this church, to those who overcome this period, "will I grant to sit with Me in My throne". This will bring us to the end of the 6th Trumpet or 6 years of Trumpets, which was Matthew group's portion. It would be interesting to read about this in Matthew. So let's have a look.

Matthew 19:28-29 *(KJV)*
28 And Jesus said unto them, Verily I say unto you, That ye which have followed me, in the ***regeneration(G3824)*** when the Son of man *shall sit in the throne of his glory*, ***ye also shall sit upon twelve thrones, judging the twelve tribes of Israel***.
29 And every one that hath forsaken houses, or

> brethren, or sisters, or father, or mother, or wife, or children, or lands, for my name's sake, shall receive an hundredfold, and shall inherit everlasting life.

Regeneration **(G3824)** **rebirth** (the state or the act), that is, (figuratively) spiritual renovation; **specifically Messianic restoration**:

Meaning when the Lord will have returned in a type of "rebirth" in the Messianic restoration of all things! They will be sitting on thrones given to them with the Lord Himself.

Over and over again, book after book, portion after portion, not one jot or tittle out of place. ALL revealing the same thing. The books have opened, the understanding is true and the time period Is 14 years. I pray this will have blessed you in understanding Him more, as it has me and many others. Another mystery revealed for a time of understanding such as this.

CHAPTER 7

THE BOOKS HAVE OPENED

This chapter is what I have come to call the "Chapters to Years". It will not be the complete revelation of each and every "Chapter to Year" in the revelation. That on its own would be a very large book. But we are going to focus on several I believe are of greater importance to understand. This will at the same time teach you how to look at all the other books that have opened. You will be able to discern some of the events that will be coming on the earth during their appointed times in the end. Being prepared and not being caught off guard or deceived.

**See the one page chart of all these opened books to their years, in the Appendix at the end of this book for an easy reference.*

These books can only be understood in this light with what we call, "End Time eyes", which is why this chapter is found later in this book. Prayerfully you have come into those "eyes" in understanding the previous revelations we have discussed. My focus will be on some of the main points to prove to you that indeed the books have opened and are speaking in a revelation of "Chapters to Years". There are no coincidences in the Word of God. Meaning they are revealing information, within each chapter, about events we have come to understand that will happen during specific years. Some even in the same chapter number. All these revelations began to open up once the two most important pieces had been revealed. Those were found in chapter one and two, with regard to whom the gospels are speaking to and the 14 years. Without those Two Keys the door to understanding the End Times with greater clarity, could have never happened.

Now let's have a look at this chart that we call the "Chapters to Years". You will notice along the top of the chart 10 books listed from the Bible. It did not start with all of them right away when this first started to be revealed to me. It has been a process that I was only able to unfold as the 14 years became more and more clear. You will also notice there are two rows to the left for 22 years and another for 15 years. I will start by first briefly explaining the 22 year connection, as it has already been covered in great detail in chapter two about the 14 Years, "*When the Years Just Don't Add Up*".

Everything will be over and restored including the final Jubilee, which is the 22nd year or the same as saying the 15th year, as you will see at the bottom of both their rows. This is the big picture. These 22 years are connected to the Hebrew alphabet, which has 22 letters. The beginning of the story from year one is given to us in Genesis 29 - 31. The story of Jacob working for his two wives and cattle, as discussed in chapter two. In Genesis 29 we see he worked 7 years before he received anything. This first 7 years I call, "the working for the Bride years", during which the Holy Spirit prepares the Bride to be ready for the Escape.

The moment Jacob had completed his first 7 years, not a day before, but immediately after, he went to his father in law for his bride. Once the wedding celebration was over, His father in law also gave him his second daughter, Rachel, who he really wanted in the first place. However, he was told he had to work still another 7 years before she would officially be his. The start of this second set of 7 years would have been the 8th year through to the end of the 14th year. When looking at the chart, you will notice that the end of the first 7 years is directly in line with the timeframe right before the 14 years begin, which is when Jacob got his first wife. You will notice the 8th year or year one is when the 14 years begin. From the start of the 8th year to the end of the 14th year in Jacob's story is giving us a type and shadow of the timeframe of the first 7 years of Seals. After this, Jesus will get the ones He came for in the first place, just as Jacob did having completed his second set of 7 years. Finally Jacob worked 6 more years for the cattle, which brings us to the end of 20 years or on the 14 year portion of the chart, which we can also see as the end of the 13th year. Both equaling the same timeframe. At the end of this time, his father in law makes a covenant with him. This is where his story ends. Remember how it ended with a covenant after 20/13 years? This will be a theme you will see connected to the time of the Lord's return feet down on the Mount of Olives at the end of the 6th trumpet, the start of the 7th trumpet timeframe. This will be the beginning of the 21st/14th year. Once the final year of Trumpets ends, it will be the final year when all the tribes will return each to receive their lands in what will be called, The Final Jubilee! - the 22nd/15th year.

And for those wondering, these final 7,7,7 years were the last three in the final Jubilee count of 7 x 7 or 49 years and 50th Jubilee. The end of the Lord 2000 years since His death and resurrection!

I will try to be as detailed as I can after having laid some groundwork. Right along the top of the chart you will see John, Genesis, and Judges as the only ones that cover the 21 years. Our focus will be on John and Genesis from chapters 1 - 21 to begin this incredible revelation. The "beginning" of it all from year 1, is the End Time connection of chapters to years for **Genesis 1:1** and **John 1:1** where both start by telling us -"In the beginning...". Or in this case, the beginning of the end days when the first set of 7 years began. Now let's see how this really proves itself out going forward. "In the beginning" was simply giving us the connection between Genesis and John. The first 7 chapters/ years, I call "the easy years" referring to Jacob saying that the days went fast when he worked for the one he loved. This is the time where the Holy Spirit has been working hard to bring in and prepare the Gentile Bride for the escape.

So now if we go to chapters 7 into 8 of Genesis we should then be able to see this type and shadow of someone that could represent the Gentile Bride or Luke's group being protected or taken. Of course, what do we know about the conversation in those chapters? It is the story of Noah and the ark. Very fitting isn't it?

> ***Genesis 7:7 and 10*** *(KJV)*
> **7** And Noah went in, and his sons, and his wife,

and his sons' wives with him, into the ark, because of the waters of the flood.

10 And it came to pass after seven days, that the waters of the flood were upon the earth.

When we get into chapter 8 we see the incredible connection explained in a previous chapter about the storyline of the 40 days coming to an end, and the remaining two sets of 7 days as years.

Genesis 8:6-9 *(KJV)*

6 And it came to pass at the end of forty days, that Noah opened the window of the ark which he had made:

7 And he sent forth a raven, which went forth to and fro, until the waters were dried up from off the earth.

8 Also he sent forth a dove from him, to see if the waters were abated from off the face of the ground;

9 But the dove found no rest for the sole of her foot, and she returned unto him into the ark, for the waters were on the face of the whole earth: then he put forth his hand, and took her, and pulled her in unto him into the ark.

As you know by now, this represents the Son of Man's 40 days, followed by the raven**(H6158)**, which actually represents the antichrist spirit going out after the Son of Man's time is over. Then the Holy Ghost as the dove goes out at Pentecost, the 50th day, followed by the 14 years!

Raven **(H6158)** From H6150; a raven (from its dusky hue) from H6150 ʿârab

And how does John 8 compare with a type and shadow of a Gentile Bride being saved?

John 8:3-10 *(KJV)*
3 And the scribes and Pharisees brought unto him
a woman taken in **adultery (G3430)**; and when
they had set her in the midst,
4 They say unto him, Master, this woman was
taken in adultery, in the very act.
5 Now Moses in the law commanded us, that such
should be stoned: but what sayest thou?
6 This they said, tempting him, that they might
have to accuse him. But Jesus stooped down, and
with his finger wrote on the ground, as though he
heard them not.
7 So when they continued asking him, he lifted up
himself, and said unto them, He that is without sin
among you, let him first cast a stone at her.
8 And **again he stooped down**, and wrote on the
ground.
9 And they which heard it, being convicted by their
own conscience, went out one by one, beginning at
the eldest, even unto the last: **and Jesus was left
alone**, and ***the woman standing in the midst.***
10 When Jesus had lifted up himself, and ***saw
none but the woman***, he said unto her, Woman,
where are those thine accusers? hath no man
condemned thee?

We have this woman standing in front of Jesus and her accusers surrounding her, leaving one by one. Only Jesus remains, with her standing before Him, still bent over having been writing on the ground and as He lifts Himself up, "*He sees no one but her*"!

It does not get any more visual with words than that! Christ down on a knee with His Gentile Bride standing in the midst of Him, and Him seeing none but her as He rises. Now that is a very clear type and shadow. Some of you may be saying, "But she is being called an adulterer?" Let's look into the understanding of that word.

Adultery **(G3430)** adultery: - adultery.

Not much there though to help us understand how she could represent the Gentile Bride, or at least not on the surface. However, we do have a beautiful story in the Old Testament of a woman who was and is still called the Gentile Bride. Her name is Ruth. She even has her own book in the Bible. So let us go see if we can find a connection to her and this woman in John 8.

> ***Ruth 2:10*** *(KJV)*
> **10** Then she fell on her face, and bowed herself to the ground, and said unto him, Why have I found grace in thine eyes, that thou shouldest take knowledge of me, *seeing I am a* ***stranger*** **(H5237)** *?*

Ruth, this Gentile bride to be of Boaz, the kinsman redeemer, calls herself a **stranger**. So let us see what this word means.

Stranger **(H5237)** applications (foreign, non-relative, **adulterous**, different, wonderful): - alien, foreigner, outlandish, strange (-r, woman).

This word "adulterous" it turns out is also a term used for a woman who is a foreigner, meaning Gentile. It sounds harsh to us, but it is the same as when Jesus called the woman in Mark 7 a dog. An adulterer can and is also used to describe a Gentile woman. This IS the type and shadow of John 8.

At this point in the 8th day/year we are now at the 1st year of the 14 years of the tribulation about to begin. Let's have a look at some more books that equal this same time. We will start with Hosea and Zechariah and bring them into the big picture. You will notice first that both of the books are exactly 14 chapters long and they are the only ones in the Bible with 14 chapters. That was what first caught my attention and then I realized that it was understood that one is written to the Gentiles and the other to the Jews/Judah. Let me start by showing with scripture that Hosea is in fact the one written to the Gentiles. Once again, it does not get any clearer than this. We discussed this in the chapter called *"When the Years Just Don't Add up"*, but I will just briefly refresh your memory.

> ***Romans 9:24-25*** *(KJV)*
> **24** Even us, whom he hath called, not of the Jews only, but also of the Gentiles?
> **25** As he saith also in **Osee (G5617)**, I will call them my people, *which were not my people*; *and her beloved, which was not beloved.*

Osee **(G5617)** Of Hebrew origin [H1954]; Hosee (that is, Hoshea), an Israelite: - Osee.

Hosea **(H1954)** means - Deliverer

It tells us the book of Hosea is written to the Gentiles, but more than that, He will call her His Beloved, who was not His Beloved before! As discussed previously, Hosea is a type and shadow of Jesus as "deliverer". Exactly what Hosea's name means. So now what does Hosea, the deliverer, tell us in the beginning of his book that shows a Gentile bride being taken?

> ***Hosea 1:2*** *(KJV)*
> **2.** The beginning of the word of the LORD by Hosea. And **the LORD said to *Hosea***, Go, take unto thee ***a wife of whoredoms*** (recall the woman in John 8, the word means adultery) and children of whoredoms: for the land hath committed great whoredom, departing from the LORD.

*This **IS** the Her Beloved from Romans 9 that He said was not His beloved, **but now she will be**.*

Again right at the start of 14 chapters, exactly where it should be in the understanding to make sense and the exact same position of chapters to years as John 8 and Genesis 8. **Jesus the "Deliverer" getting His Gentile Bride!**

We also read as a further confirmation about this Gentile Bride in the book of Acts. Without going into everything the book of Acts shows us about all its chapters to years, let's have a look at one in particular.

Act 15:14 – 15 *(KJV)*
14 Simeon hath declared how God at the first did visit the Gentiles, *to take out of them a people for his name.*
15 And to this agree the words of the prophets; as it is written...

You can clearly see from the chart that the book of Acts has opened to us by dividing into two sets of 14 years view. Chapter 15 is also in that first place again as each of the others are. We see that God came to take out a group from among the Gentiles for Himself. We are told the words of the prophets agree to this, and where was it just shown to you from... a prophet. How amazing is that!

Here is a good place to let you also know that just because something happens in a chapter to any year, it does not always mean it is going to be at the start of that year. It could very well be the middle or even the end of the year, that that discussion is referring to. It is the understanding of the End Times scriptures that gives us the discernment. For example, in what we have discussed, it is easy to understand, because we know the Gentile Bride is removed right near the start of the 14 years. Here is another thing to consider as well. The end of a year and the start of another are essentially the same time, as they are connected to each other, meaning where the one ends, the other begins. The same thing was happening here with these chapters. They are simply showing us the Gentile Bride is taken right near the beginning.

Now let's quickly turn our attention to Judah. As discussed before, just as Hosea was clearly written to the Gentiles for the End Times, so is Zechariah and his 14 chapters to years written to the Jews/ Judah. We know that Israel/Jerusalem will be attacked first and then destroyed right around the start of the tribulation as well. Recall how we spoke in a previous chapter about the 50 years of having the land of Jerusalem, they have been disobedient, never having allowed the land to rest it's sabbath years, even once? That means it must be destroyed and them removed from the land, because it must remain vacant of them for 7 years before the Lord can allow the rebuilding to begin. And we know that time, as well as the end of the true 70th year, is literally just about up as I write this. You may even be reading this after it has happened. So knowing this for Israel/Jerusalem, let's see what we read happens to them in their beginning, in Zechariah 1.

Let me start with a little reminder we covered in Daniel 9. We read about an attack happening during the middle verses, before the 14 years began. If you recall the 14 years will begin at Pentecost or Feast of "Weeks" as Daniel 9:24 explained. We see how in Daniel 9:2 he told us that it would "accomplish 70 years in the desolations". So let's have a read of Zechariah 1.

> ***Zechariah 1:12, 14-15*** *(KJV)*
> **12** Then the angel of the LORD answered and said, O LORD of hosts, how long wilt thou not have mercy *on Jerusalem and on the cities of Judah*, against which thou hast had indignation ***these threescore and ten years?***

14 So the angel that communed with me said unto
me, Cry thou, saying, Thus saith the LORD of hosts;
I am *jealous for Jerusalem* and for Zion with a great
jealousy.
15 And I am very sore displeased with the heathen
that are at ease: for I was but a little displeased, and
they helped forward **the affliction (H7451)**.

Remember how GOD is angry with them for not allowing the land to rest during those Sabbaths? Look at what He says in verse 12. "How long before you will have mercy *"on Jerusalem and the cities of Judah"*. He is NOT speaking about the people. He is talking about the land and He is about to remove them from it. There it is again... "***These"*** ***70***/*threescore and ten* ***years***, which means at some point in the 70th year, as we have been able to discern, we are right near the end of it.

Affliction **(H7451)** means evil, distress, sore, sorrow, trouble, vex, wicked (-ly, -ness, one), worse (-st) wretchedness, wrong.

This is the start of tribulation, war and destruction will begin in Israel. When you continue reading into verses 18-21, you see that they have all been scattered. All still in chapter 1.

I have one more book I wanted to include in this chapter. And that is the book of Psalms. It was noticed, I believe back in the 1980's, to have had types and shadows of events to years within them and believed to have begun its count in 1900 or 1901. However, most believed it ended in the year 1999. While others still tried to say it kept going, but were having a hard time showing this same flow as earlier years. They would tell us it puts us in chapter 121 now (as we are in 2021 as of this writing). However, that is not accurate as I will now show you.

As the books began to open to me this was one I really started to look at closely. I soon realized it was not happening in line with the years. Meaning just because it was 118 did not mean it was 20"18". I realized that there was a dual grouping like we saw in the book of Acts earlier, and that it started with chapter 18 and 118. Now when you read chapter 18 you realize this is a MAJOR event that has not yet taken place and that 118 was similar in its wording. Psalm 118 however did skip the details of the major event on earth and also spoke about something else happening at that time. I soon realized chapter 18 was speaking to the event that was going to begin right before the 14 years of Seals and Trumpets started, which then made Psalms 19/119 to 32/132 the End Time chapters to years and made 33/133 the final Jubilee year, as you have come to understand as the 22nd/15th year at the end. See the chart and how Psalms has two columns starting with 18 and 118. You will notice that the first two fall in line with "before" the tribulation begins. After having taught on this for a few months, I received an email from someone who shared with me that there was this grouping of Psalms called "Song of Ascents", a title given ***to fifteen of the Psalms***, 120–134 (119–133 in the Septuagint and the Vulgate). Now the 119 to 133 of course caught my attention. The Septuagint was in fact the correct one for us, as it was the Original Hebrew to Greek translation.

Back to their meaning, quoted from:

https://en.wikipedia.org/wiki/Song_of_Ascents:
"these psalms were sung by worshippers as they ascended the road to Jerusalem to attend the three pilgrim festivals"

It turned out they were an exact type and shadow as these were sung at ***THREE ASCENTS*** *or goings up* ***to be with the LORD*** in Jerusalem. Or you could say in the End Times understanding - Escape, Rapture, Return! What an incredible confirmation it was. So now let me show a little of what it says in the Psalms 18, which comes just before the 14 years begins.

> ***Psalms 18:6-16, 19-20*** *(KJV)*
> **6** In my distress I called upon the LORD, and cried unto my God: he heard my voice out of his temple, and my cry came before him, even into his ears.
> **7** Then the earth shook and trembled; the foundations also of the hills moved and were shaken, *because he was wroth.*
> **8** There went up a smoke out of his nostrils, and fire out of his mouth devoured: coals were kindled by it.
> **9** He bowed the heavens also, ***and came down***: and darkness was under his feet.
> **10** And he rode upon a cherub, and did fly: yea, he did fly upon the wings of the wind.
> **11** He made darkness his secret place; his pavilion round about him were dark waters and thick clouds of the skies.
> **12** At the brightness that was before him his thick clouds passed, **hail stones and coals of fire**.
> **13** The LORD also thundered in the heavens, and

the Highest gave his voice; **<u>hail stones and coals of fire</u>**.

14 Yea, <u>he sent out his arrows, and scattered them</u>; and he shot out lightnings, and discomfited them.

15 Then <u>the channels of waters were seen, and the foundations of the world were discovered</u> at thy rebuke, O LORD, at the blast of the breath of thy nostrils.

16 *<u>He sent from above, **he took me, he drew me out of many waters**.</u>*

19 He <u>brought me forth also into a large place</u>; ***he delivered me, because he delighted in me***.

20 The LORD rewarded me according to my righteousness; *<u>according to **the cleanness of my hands (H3027)**</u>* hath he recompensed me.

Cleanness **(H1252)** From H1305; <u>purity</u>: - cleanness, pureness.

Hands **(H3027)** <u>a hand</u> (the open one (<u>indicating power</u>, means, direction.

You will see in a later chapter the reason I show these words for "hands" and "cleanness" here. They are not going to have the same meaning.

Do you recall what Acts 15:14 told us a little earlier in the exact same place on the chart? <u>How GOD did at first "visit" the Gentiles to "take out" a people for His name</u>. Consider what is happening here amidst this chaos at His approach.

I have to stop myself here for a moment, because I have so many places I can go into to show how the End Times are played out within all the different parts of all these opened books listed on the chart. But I will stay on track with my plan for this chapter. So with that said, let's look forward to a few years/chapters, towards the end of the 6th seal timeframe, as well as the 7th year sabbath of Seals and the first year of Trumpets. These are the chapters to years on the chart of 13, 14 and 15 in the 22 year column or 6, 7 and 8 in the 15 year column.

I said earlier I would also show you more in Hosea. Remember, Hosea speaks to the Gentiles. And even though the Bride was taken at the start, the Bride was not the whole church, as we have discussed in the chapter of "*Who Are The Gospels Speaking To?"* Only the ready, watching and praying were the Bride. The rest of Hosea is still speaking to the sleeping church, the left behind/MARK group. In Hosea 6 we see what those having made it through 6 years of the Seals are saying.

> ***Hosea 6:1 - 3*** *(KJV)*
> **1** Come, and let us *return* unto the LORD: for he hath torn, and he will heal us; he hath smitten, and he will bind us up.
> **2** ***After two days*** will he **revive** us: in **the third day** he will raise us up, *and we shall live in his sight*
> **3** Then shall we know, if we follow on to know the LORD:

They are saying that they have endured harsh tribulation, "So let us return to Him", which is the time of the end of the 6th year. So how is it they will return to Him? Remember they will have seen Him coming on Mount Zion and what soon follows will be the rapture. They are saying that after 2 days or in reality 2000 years the LORD will bring them back after His return feet down at the end and in 3 days or 3000 years, which is when the 1000 years are finished. Saying, "We will be raised to life and know whether we will go on to live with Him forever."

Let's have a quick look to see what we find in Psalms at this same period of time.

> ***Psalms 24:1-4*** *(KJV)*
> **1** A Psalm of David. The earth is the LORD'S, and **the fulness** thereof; the world, and they that dwell therein.
> **2** For he hath founded it upon the seas, and established it upon the floods.
> **3** **Who shall** *ascend into* ***the hill of the LORD***? or who shall stand in his holy place?
> **4** *He that hath* ***clean (H5355) hands (H3709)***, and a pure heart; who hath not lifted up his soul unto vanity, nor sworn deceitfully.

What comes at the end of the 6th year/seal? The LORD coming on Mount Zion, the "HILL of the LORD". And when this happens it will also be the end of the times of the Gentiles, which is also called; "**THE FULNESS** of the Gentiles come in" or the coming end of Mark's group at the rapture.

Who does it say at this time will be able to go up this Hill of the LORD. Those with "clean" "hands" Let's compare them to the other two earlier.

Clean **(H5355)** <u>From H5352</u>; innocent: - blameless, clean, clear, exempted from H5352 to be <u>(or **make)** **clean**</u> (literally or figuratively);

So unlike the first group in chapter 18. This group had to be made or make themselves clean. And how did that happen? Through their enduring faith through much tribulation.

And how about their "hands"?

Hands **(H3709)** the hollow <u>hand or palm</u> (<u>**the leaves of a palm tree**</u>); - **branch**

The word in chapter 18 was a hand of power. Whereas this one speaks of a hand holding a palm "branch".

This should ring a bell from the chapter *"The 40 Days of the Son of Man"*. We spoke about how the dove when it goes out the second time in Genesis 8:10-11, returns with a "branch" in its mouth "pluckt off", which was shown as a type and shadow of the rapture group. We are seeing the same thing here. Here it is a little more specific in the sense that we are reading "it is about" to happen, not that it has happened yet. This is why it says "who <u>shall</u> ascend", as if to say the time is just about at hand. Let me now show you this group with palms in their hands, having "**ascended**" and now before Him. It is found in Revelation 7, which is literally speaking to this same rapture group, but now having been raptured in the 7th year.

Revelation 7:9-10, 14 *(KJV)*
9 After this I beheld, and, lo, <u>a great multitude, which no man could number, of all nations, and</u>

kindreds, and people, and tongues, stood before the throne, and before the Lamb, clothed with white robes, **and palms in their hands**;
10 And cried with a loud voice, saying, Salvation to our God which sitteth upon the throne, and unto the Lamb.
14 And I said unto him, Sir, thou knowest. And he said to me, These are they which came out of great tribulation, and **have washed their robes**, and **made them white (G3021)** in the blood of the Lamb.

As you can see this is the group that has the "have palms in their hands" and they made them white **(G3021)** to whiten: - **make white**, whiten.

This is that same group from Psalms 24 that is now before Him having washed themselves clean and have palms in their hands.

We are going to remain for the next few points in the same timeframe as the 7th year of Seals, with the Lord having come down on Mount Zion and Him gathering them to him, as we look at the other books.

To start we will keep in this Gentile line of thought, starting with John 14, which if you look at the chart again you will see it is the 7th year of Seals.

John 14:2-3 *(KJV)*
2 In my Father's house are many mansions: if it were not so, I would have told you. I go to prepare a place for you.
3 And if I go and prepare a place for you, ***I will***

***come again*, and *receive you unto myself*; that *where I am, there ye may be also*.**

This is a clear type and shadow reference to when He will come down on the mountain carved without hands, which is paradise and will "receive" unto Himself, His "rapture" group, into the place He has prepared, paradise. These chapters do not once fail to reveal in relation to an event or events during any of the End Time years, as they should.

Genesis 14:18-20 *(KJV)*
18 And **Melchizedek (H4442)** king of Salem
brought forth bread and wine: and he was **the
priest of the most high God**.
19 And he blessed him, and said, Blessed be
Abram of the most high God, possessor of heaven
and earth:
20 And blessed be the most high God, which hath
delivered thine enemies into thy hand. And he gave
him tithes of all.

Here in the chapter to year for the 7th year of Seals, we find for the first time in the Bible the name Melchizedek. If any of you reading have heard teaching about him before, you will know that he is a type and shadow of Jesus. Melchizedek the high priest, is another name for Jesus, our High Priest. The meaning of the name is: Melchizedek **(H4442)** means, king of right.

And this chapter is telling us that GOD has delivered his enemies into His hand. How does that reference fit? When the Lord comes at the end of the 6th year of Seals, He will destroy the antichrist and false prophet system that had taken over the world with the mark of the beast spoken about in a previous chapter. It is the same reference from Daniel 2 about the stone that will crush the image and become a great mountain. This is speaking of the Lord on Mount Zion. At this point, let me show Him to you in the book of Revelation literally standing on it.

> ***Revelation 14:1*** *(KJV)*
> **1** And I looked, and, lo, **a Lamb <u>stood on the mount Sion</u>**, and with him an hundred forty and four thousand, having his Father's name written in their foreheads.

Now you can understand why the Lamb is standing on Mount Zion in this chapter. And the reason He is there with the 144,000 who were sealed from Chapter 7 of Revelation, is because they are about to begin their evangelising at the start of Trumpets. The Lord being there has caused many people to wonder for generations how this was possible when we have all been taught He does not return until feet down on the Mount of Olives, at the end of it all. A big mystery is what this coming on Mount Zion is going to look like. It is certainly going to be terrifying as we see people hiding in caves, crying out at the end of the 6th seal for the rocks and mountains to fall on them, wow!

Next, in Zechariah 7 we are given more understanding as to the timing in this place of the 7th seal. The Lord is rehashing why He scattered them back then throughout this chapter. He lets us know that the 7 years that Jerusalem had to remain vacant is not over quite yet.

Wait until we get into Zechariah 8 and forward. The conversation will then have strongly turned to the Jews/Judah, which will begin their 7 years, after having been removed for the first 7 years during Seals judgment.

Zechariah 7:5-7 *(KJV)*

5 Speak unto all the people of the land, and to the priests, saying, **When** ye **fasted** and **mourned** in the fifth and seventh month, even ***those seventy years***, did ye at all fast unto me, even to me?
6 And when ye did eat, and when ye did drink, did not ye eat for yourselves, and drink for yourselves?
7 Should ye not hear the words which the LORD hath cried by the former prophets, **when** Jerusalem **was inhabited** and in prosperity, and the cities thereof round about her, **when men inhabited** the south and the plain?

It is ALL past tense, including "those", and here it is again, 70 years! Another one of those very clear pieces of End Time scriptures. This chapter represents the final 7th year of them having been removed.

As we begin to close out this first set of 7 years, in the chapters to years. We are going to go with Psalms 25 and 125. Both of them have the same year representation on the chart, the 7th year of Seals. The first will show you the same Mountain again right in its place. But then the other, although in the same year, is a different message.

Psalm 125:1-2 *(KJV)*

1 They that trust in the LORD shall be as mount

Zion, which cannot be removed, but abideth forever.
2 As the mountains are round about Jerusalem, so the LORD is round about his people from henceforth even for ever.

Psalm 25:10, 13-14 *(KJV)*
10 All the paths of the LORD are mercy and truth unto such as keep **his covenant** and his testimonies.
13 His soul shall dwell at ease; and *his seed shall inherit the earth*.
14 The secret of the LORD is with them that fear him; and **he will** shew them **his covenant (H1285)**.

You will notice there is now this conversation about a covenant that He is about to make with them as they come into the land, which in the End Time understanding is about to end the first 7 years, when they are literally going to be coming back into the land with the Lord on Mount Zion. You will see this very clearly as we move into the next chapter to year. What is also interesting is that the 7th seal in Revelation 8 does not tell us too much, but it does tell us, for one, that it is a short period of time, which in heaven is called "about, half an hour". After all my studies and understanding of the End Times in the opened books, I believe this period of time on earth is going to be "about 6 months". Now lining up with the first portion of the 7th year of Seals, which was chapter 7 of Revelation, being about 6 months as well, this gives us a full year. Remember, as I stated earlier, it is not one seal per year. But there is more to this "about 6 months" of the 7th seal. That is that the word "silence"(G4602) means silence or hush and comes from (G4623), which also means be calm and to Hold Peace! I believe during this period of the 7th seal is when the Lord is going to be making His covenant with all, as you will understand and see much more clearly in a little bit.

Covenant **(H1285)** a compact, confederacy, [con-]feder[-ate], covenant, league.

This word for covenant found here in Psalms 25 is the same as seen in Genesis 15:18. Even though this word is used a number of times in scripture, you must consider the context it is found in. In both of these cases, they are both speaking of the same thing at the same time in their chapter to year understanding. What are the odds of that? This is, "when they will come into the land the Lord will give them again" Now as we move into the first year of Trumpets on the chart, let's start with this Genesis 15 conversation to see what we are talking about.

> ***Genesis 15:7, 18*** *(KJV)*
> **7** And he said unto him, I am the LORD that brought thee out of Ur of the Chaldees, ***to give thee this land to inherit it.***
> **18** In **the same day the LORD** ***made a covenant*** with Abram, saying, Unto thy seed **have I given this land**, from the river of Egypt unto the great river, the river Euphrates:

We see He has in this chapter to year now brought them into the land and made the covenant. Just as He will do when He comes on Mount Zion and then in the first year of Trumpets begin the rebuilding of Jerusalem. As I had mentioned, this is when everything for the Jews/Judah really gets going again, because they had been removed and shattered for the first 7 years during the time of the Gentiles. But that period is now over, it is their time again, known as "Jacob's Trouble". We see right away in Zechariah 8, that it is the 8th year since the tribulation started or the first year of Trumpets time, as was Genesis 15.

> ***Zechariah 8:2-3*** *(KJV)*
> **2** Thus saith the LORD of hosts; **I was** jealous for Zion with great jealousy, and **I was** jealous for her with great fury.

(remember in chapter 1 the LORD said "**I am**" jealous, yet now it's "**I was**" and the reason is because...)

> **3** Thus saith the LORD; *I am returned unto Zion*, and will dwell in the midst of Jerusalem: and Jerusalem shall be called a city of truth; *and **the mountain of the LORD of hosts** the holy mountain*.

He has returned on the mountain carved without hands, which became the Holy Mount Zion, the mountain of the LORD now established in Jerusalem, which is why we saw in Revelation 14, as mentioned earlier, the Lamb was on it with the 144,000 ready to be sent out. The Lord is now established at the beginning of Trumpets in Jerusalem and will now remain there for the next 3.5 years or the first half of Trumpets, while the city, streets, wall and temple are being rebuilt.

But now let's see what else Zechariah 8 has to say to support this.

> ***Zechariah 8:9-10*** *(KJV)*
> **9** Thus saith the LORD of hosts; **Let your hands be strong,** ye that hear in these days these words by the mouth of the prophets, which were in the day that the foundation of the house of the LORD of hosts was laid, ***that the temple might be built.***
> **10** For **before these days** there was no hire for man, nor any hire for beast; **neither was there any peace** to him that went out or came in, because of the **affliction (H6862)**: for **I set all men every one against his neighbour.**

Affliction **(H6862)** distress, enemy, flint, foe, narrow, small, sorrow, strait, tribulation, trouble.

We see Him telling them to be ready with strong hands, because the rebuilding of the temple is about to begin. This is the same time we were reading in Daniel 9:25-26 when the rebuilding for the next 3.5 years would begin with Messiah there. Listen to what He tells them the reason was as to why they could not build the temple sooner. He tells them because "peace" was gone, the "affliction" which literally means the tribulation had begun, and that at that time, He "set all men everyone against his neighbour". When do we know all men will be set against each other? Right at the beginning of tribulation. Just as we see in each of the Olivet discourses in Luke, Mark and Matthew. When it begins, it will be "nation against nation, kingdom against kingdom'', which is the time of the "great sword" brought about by the Red Horse rider of the second seal when "peace" is removed.

> ***Revelation 6:4*** *(KJV)*
> **4** And there went out *<u>another horse that was red</u>*: and <u>power was given to him</u> that sat thereon **<u>to take peace from the earth</u>**, and **<u>that they should kill one another</u>**: and <u>there was given unto him a great sword</u>.

Pretty clear as to when it all began, when the LORD is telling them this in Zechariah 8:10. At the beginning of tribulation for the first 7 years.

In just these few (and there were quite a few) scriptures of the opened books revelation, I have confirmed the following all lining up in the chapters to years understanding:

- the timeframe of the Escape of the Gentile Bride,
- the beginning and end of the tribulation of Seals, including the rapture,
- when the Lord is seen coming at the end of the 6th seal,
- that He first comes down on Mount Zion, the mountain carved without hands to receive His rapture group.
- As well as when He will make a new covenant, and Israel/Jerusalem will begin to get rebuilt including the temple.

We have an awesome GOD!

Let's go from the beginning of Trumpets to the middle of Trumpets. We understand during the first half of

Trumpets things are getting rebuilt and the 144,000 are out evangelising. At this point it is about to get even crazier than the earth has ever seen, even compared to the Seals that had recently passed, with the time of WWIII and the antichrist. This is where it is going to get so unbelievably difficult that I have a hard time understanding who could endure this period, but we know some do!

This period again, is the **very important** halfway point of Trumpets. The rebuilding will have happened and the temple will have been completed. This brings us to a total of 10.5 years to date since the tribulation began. We know this time well from a couple places like Revelation 12:9, the point at which satan will have lost his battle against Michael and his angels and be cast down to earth with his fallen angels. As well as the same time of Revelation 9:1, the time of the 5th trumpet, when the angel comes down and the pit is opened. We will cover these points in greater detail in the following chapter called *"Revealing Revelation"*.

At this point those 10.5 years should sound very familiar to you. You may recall them from the Daniel 9 chapter, the timeframe referred to in Daniel 9:26 where Messiah will be cut off. The only way Messiah could be cut off is if satan was here. You will also recall this is the same year total from Psalms 90:10 at the time of "we fly away". I have just given four references to this period, but let me show you this time of Him being "cut off" in the chapters to years book that speaks to this time of the Jews/Judah, in Zechariah. For this to be in Zechariah reflected as 3.5

years into Trumpets, it must be in chapter 11 and no other. And that is exactly where it is!

Zechariah 11:1- 2 *(KJV)*
1 Open thy doors, O Lebanon, that the fire may devour thy cedars.
2 Howl, fir tree; *for the cedar is fallen*; because the mighty are spoiled: howl, O ye oaks of Bashan; **for the forest of the vintage is come down.**

Satan has lost his battle and has been cast down to earth. He is the vintage come down. Remember there were giants before the flood and after that according to **Genesis 6.** They were also referred to as cedar trees for their size. This is going to be a horrific period of time for any left on the earth. Let's continue reading in chapter 11.

Zechariah 11:9 - 10 *(KJV)*
9 Then said I, I will not feed you: that that dieth, let it die; and that that is to be cut off, let it be cut off; and let the rest eat every one the flesh of another.

(horrific as stated)

10 And I took my staff, even Beauty, and cut it asunder, that I might **break my covenant** *which I had made* ***with all the people***.

This is where Messiah must break the covenant He made with many, because satan has now been cast down to the earth. The Lord cannot keep His covenant going during this period. But do not forget this is also the point now in Revelation 12:14 when those who were there with the Lord will be protected, which is the remnant that "fly away" of Psalm 90:10. Having flown into the wilderness on the wings of an eagle until all is passed, right to the very end of all tribulation. You will recall in Daniel 9 this period of time with satan's rule will last 2.5 years, until the Lord returns once and for all as lightning from heaven after now a total of 13 years (or 20 years in the big picture) have passed. This final 14th year that Jesus comes at the beginning to fulfill Himself has been detailed in a number of scriptures earlier in the book. Let me finish proving out these books in their chapters to years right to the end of the tribulation.

> ***Zechariah 14:4, 12*** *(KJV)*
> **4** And ***his feet shall stand in that day upon the mount of Olives***, which is before Jerusalem on the east, and the mount of Olives shall cleave in the midst thereof toward the east and toward the west, and there shall be a very great valley; and half of the mountain shall remove toward the north, and half of it toward the south.

And here is a little of what Jesus is going to do during this final year to all those who came against Jerusalem.

> **12** And this shall be the plague wherewith the LORD will smite all the people that have fought against Jerusalem; **Their flesh shall consume away while they stand upon their feet, and their eyes shall consume away in their holes, and their tongue shall consume away in their mouth**.

This is happening during the final 7th year of Trumpets or 14th year since the start of tribulation or the 21st year of the big picture, while those who were taken into the wilderness with eagle's wings are still being kept until this year is over.

This also means if Jesus has returned feet down on the Mount of Olives after 13 years, it is also the time of the 2 days or in reality 2000 years to His return from His death and resurrection. Let's have a quick look at the chart again and see what year it was at the end of the 13th year when He returns feet down. The end of that year is the end of the year 2033! Exactly 2000 years from when He left after His death and resurrection in 33AD and as we were told He would return feet down on the Mount of Olives as He left in Acts 1!

Now some of you may have noticed on the chart that that year says 2033/34 when Jesus returns feet down. The reason for this is for those counting a year from January to December on a Gregorian calendar. The Gregorian calendar was not invented until 1582. And prior to it a year had always been from spring to spring. Including GOD's word as we read the start of the year is at Nisan 1, which is always near or around the Spring equinox. As much as the world has been fouled into believing it is actually in the dead of winter, it is not, and never was before Rome changed it. GOD has not changed! So when you see the date on the chart for example as you do for 2033/34 it means from Spring 2033 to the end of 2033, right around Spring of 2034!

If you are able to, a fun study that is easy to find online is that of "April Fools Day". The story behind it is all about this calendar change by Rome and how they would shame people who had not changed to their new calendar.

> ***John 20:9*** *(KJV)*
> **9** For as yet they knew not the scripture, <u>that he must rise again from the dead</u>.

In each gospel, Jesus' resurrection is found in the last chapter. However, in John only is it found in the second last chapter. Why? Because the Lord would return again <u>after 2000 years</u> and <u>fulfill the final year Himself</u>. Just as we have been revealing with End Time eyes in the understanding why John has 21 chapters. I mentioned the end of one year is the same timeframe as the start of the next. That is exactly what applies here in John as well. In fact the reason I came to understand the end of one or beginning of another, is because it appears in some places more like He will actually return at the end of the 6th trumpet which, for example, I believe is the reason for the great earthquake at that time. Yet we can clearly know He is here at the very beginning of the 7th trumpet.

In the final 14th chapter of Hosea we find the word spoken by the people back in chapter 6, saying after 2 days (or 2000) He would "<u>revive</u>" them. There it now is in the correct chapter to year, yet again.

> ***Hosea 14:6 - 7*** *(KJV)*
> **6** His branches shall spread, and his beauty shall be as the olive tree, and his smell as Lebanon.
> **7** <u>They that dwell under his shadow **shall return**</u>; **they shall <u>revive</u>** as the corn, and grow as the vine: the scent thereof shall be as the wine of Lebanon.

Next in Genesis 21, the same year period, we see the same connection right at the start.

> ***Genesis 21:1 - 5*** *(KJV)*
> **1** And the LORD visited Sarah as he had said, and the LORD did unto Sarah as he had spoken.
> **2** For Sarah conceived, and bare Abraham a son in his old age, at the set time of which God had spoken to him.
> **3** And Abraham called the name of his son that was born unto him, whom Sarah *bare to him,* ***Isaac***.
> **4** And Abraham circumcised his son Isaac being eight days old, as God had commanded him.
> **5** And **Abraham was *an hundred years old*,** when **his son Isaac was born** unto him.

The Promise, Isaac, who we also know is a type and shadow of Jesus is born, or as we could say in our End Time understanding, is returned! Right on time. What makes this even more incredible is what we covered about this in the chapter *"When The Years Just Don't Add Up"*, when Abraham had his first son, Ishmael, he was 86 years old, and now at the Coming/Birth of Isaac, Abraham is now 100 years old, 14 years.

When He comes at that final year, *He will* **RENEW the covenant** *He made* at the start of Trumpets, which He then breaks, because of satan having been cast down. Where can we find this? One of course was covered in Daniel 9:27, but let me show you another in the chapters to years.

Psalm 132:11-14 *(KJV)*
11 The LORD hath sworn in truth unto David; he
will not turn from it; Of the fruit of thy body will I
set upon thy throne.
12 If thy children will keep **my covenant** and my
testimony that I shall *teach* them, their children
shall also sit upon thy throne for evermore.
13 For the LORD hath chosen Zion; he hath desired
it for his habitation.
14 This is my rest *for ever:* *here will I dwell; for I
have desired it.*

We see here that it is finished and He is here to stay forever right to the end of the earth. Just as the last verse of Matthew 28 says.

And finally:

With the 14 years completed and all tribulation is now over, only one thing remains. To bring those who had been protected in the wilderness for the final 3.5 years, back to Jerusalem. Upon their return it will be the final 50th year **JUBILEE**! As stated from the beginning, it will be the 22nd year or also referred to as the 15th from the tribulation years, as per the Chapters to Years chart.

Let's wrap this all up by showing it to you in one of the books we did not go into yet. That is the book of Ezekiel. It starts in the very last portion of chapter 47 and runs through all of chapter 48, the end of the Jubilee year! Then we will end it all in Psalms one last time.

Ezekiel 47:13 -15 *(KJV)*
13 Thus saith the Lord GOD; **This shall be the**

border, whereby ye shall inherit the land according to the twelve tribes of Israel: Joseph shall have two portions.
14 And ye shall inherit it, one as well as another: concerning the which I lifted up mine hand to give it unto your fathers: and this land shall fall unto you for inheritance.
15 And this shall be the border of the land toward the north side, from the great sea, the way of Hethlon, as men go to Zedad;

Ezekiel 48:1-3, 35 *(KJV)*
1 Now these are the names of the tribes. From the north end to the coast of the way of Hethlon, as one goeth to Hamath, Hazarenan, the border of Damascus northward, to the coast of Hamath; for these are his sides east and west; a portion for Dan.
2 *And by* ***the border of Dan***, from the east side unto the west side, a portion for Asher.
3 And by **the border of Asher**, from the east side even unto the west side, a portion for Naphtali.

This continues with all the remaining tribes, then verse 35.

35 It was round about eighteen thousand measures: ***and the name of the city from that day shall be, The LORD is there***.

How awesome is that!

And last but not least, Psalms 33, being at exactly the right place on the chart for the Jubilee and we read.

Psalm 33: 3-5, 8 *(KJV)*
3 Sing unto him a new song; play skillfully with a
loud noise.
4 For the word of the LORD is right; and all his
works **are done** in truth.
5 He loveth righteousness and judgment: the earth
is full of the goodness of the LORD.
8 *Let all the earth fear the LORD*: ***let all the***
inhabitants of the world *stand in awe of him*

Psalm 133:1 - 3

1 Behold, how good and how pleasant it is for
brethren to dwell together in unity!
2 It is like the precious ointment upon the head,
that ran down upon the beard, even Aaron's beard:
that went down to the skirts of his garments;
3 As the dew of Hermon, and as the dew that
descended upon the mountains of Zion: *for there*
the LORD commanded the blessing, ***even life for***
evermore.

And now in these last several scriptures I have confirmed the final set of 7 years including the Jubilee, in the understanding of the opened books, chapters to years, perfectly aligned.

- confirmed the time of Messiah's being cut off;
- the cutting off of the covenant He made with all,
- satan being cast down to the earth and his 2.5 year reign.
- when Christ will return feet down on the Mount of Olives;
- when He will renew His covenant He cut off,

- and the final Jubilee where each tribe is given their inheritance.

Believe it or not, all these are but a few examples of the revelations of the opened books, chapters to years. I had so much more I wanted to add. But these were chosen to reveal the understanding without going too far, and to catch your attention to want to dig deeper into them for yourselves. Referring to this chart, to understand events in the coming years of tribulation, I believe will be a great tool for all. Making this book a great leave behind for family and friends you love and are concerned for.

I pray this has blessed you with a greater understanding of our Lord and Saviour Jesus Christ in His coming prophetic end of days.

CHAPTER 8

REVEALING REVELATION

In this chapter I am going to cover the Tribulation from the book of Revelation, chapters 6 through 13, as well as touching on a few after them. I advise you to not skip the chapters in this book before this, as it will be overwhelming without the necessary understanding. All of it will be in order, in a detailed breakdown, which will cover many topics already discussed. All combined in one total picture of the whole Tribulation of 14 years. A complete journey through Seals and Trumpets in great detail. Once again, showing not only is it impossible for all of this to have fit into a 7 year timeframe, but also that it would have been impossible had the Books not truly been Opened!

I encourage you to read this chapter with the Tribulation TimeLine Chart in the Appendix, as well as taking your Bible out and following along with me.

THE SEALS JUDGMENT

We are going to start in Revelation 6. Looking at the Tribulation TimeLine Chart in the Appendix, you will see right at the start the horseman that will be released, which is the breaking of the seals.

Our first thought is that each of these horsemen are the representation of the beast, for example, the lion as the White Horse, the bear as Red Horse, the leopard as the

Black Horse, and the fourth beast as the Pale Horse, as we have also read in Daniel 7.

Daniel 7:3-7 *(KJV)*
3 And four great beasts came up from the sea,
diverse one from another.
4 The **first was like a lion,** and had eagle's wings: I
beheld till the wings thereof were plucked, and it
was lifted up from the earth, and made stand upon
the feet as a man, and a man's heart was given to
it.
5 And behold another beast, a **second, like to a**
bear, and it raised up itself on one side, and it had
three ribs in the mouth of it between the teeth of it:
and they said thus unto it, Arise, devour much
flesh.
6 After this I beheld, and lo **another, like a**
leopard, which had upon the back of it four wings
of a fowl; the beast had also four heads; and
dominion was given to it.
7 After this I saw in the night visions, and behold **a**
fourth beast, dreadful and terrible, and strong
exceedingly; and it had great iron teeth: it devoured
and brake in pieces, and stamped the residue with
the feet of it: and it was diverse from all the beasts
that were before it; and it had ten horns.

However, there is more than one set of events taking place. Having come to understand Zechariah's book and its timing better, let's go have a look at it again in chapter 1 and see where there is more than one set of four.

Zechariah 1:18-21 *(KJV)*

8 Then lifted I up mine eyes, and saw, and behold
four horns.

19 And I said unto the angel that talked with me,
What be these? And he answered me, These are the
horns which have scattered Judah, Israel, and
Jerusalem.

20 And the LORD shewed me four carpenters.

21 Then said I, What come these to do? And he
spake, saying, These are the horns which have
scattered Judah, so that no man did lift up his head:
but these are come to fray them, to cast out the
horns of the Gentiles, which lifted up their horn
over the land of Judah to scatter it.

Here we can see that there are two groups of four. These two groups are the difference between Daniel 7's four and Revelation 6's four. To add to this a little more, you can see in Daniel 7 that they came up from the sea. Whereas Revelation 6 they are released from heaven. The other thing we can understand is that they are essentially sent out at "about" the same time. However, this will not happen at the same time. Meaning some will do their greatest portion maybe a couple years or more later, while yet still part of one of the others. They will overlap their portion with another, while maybe one ends its portion. So although it may at times appear that it is one seal per year, it is not. They also do not all come just near the beginning and leave either. It is all over a period of time until their time is fulfilled.

What is the first that we see happening in Revelation? First of all, it is the Lamb, Jesus, who is opening the seals.

This means His 40 days as the Son of Man on earth have ended. We have established that from the end of the Son of Man's time there is still a portion of time to Pentecost when the Holy Ghost, in what we call "Acts 2.0", will baptize those who the Lord has chosen to work for Him during the Seals judgments. Once that has happened it will begin the 14 years.

The often debated question has been who the white horse rider will represent? For this we have to go back to the chapter, *"The Revelation of Daniel 9"* about 2 Chronicles 36:22-23. After the first attack in the Middle East with major destruction in Israel, it will be followed by this modern day Cyrus character. He will come on the scene and be the one to make the "declaration/decree" to allow Israel to "rebuild". Just as we covered in the Daniel 9 study. This explains to me as well why we read how the "White Horse Rider" conquers having only a "bow" yet no arrows and has a "crown". He will not do it by war, but by peace.

> ***Revelation 6:1-2*** *(KJV)*
> **1** And I <u>saw when the Lamb opened</u> one of the
> seals, and I heard, as it were the noise of thunder,
> one of the four beasts saying, Come and see.
> **2** And I saw, and behold <u>a white horse</u>: and he that
> sat on him <u>had a **bow (G5115)**; and a crown</u> was
> given unto him: and he went forth <u>conquering, and
> to conquer</u>.

Bow **(G5115)** a bow (apparently as <u>the simplest fabric</u>): - bow.

As we can see it is not a weapon, but simple fabric, very possibly like paper for this decree of peace to rebuild, to be written on?

Although the two sets of four go out very close to each other, they do the greater part of work at their appropriate times. We see that this peace declaration/decree will be short lived. In Daniel 9:25 we read what follows the decree - the first 7 weeks/years, which represented the 7 years Jerusalem would then remain vacant and the beginning of the whole 14 years. So the question is what will happen right around the time of that decree? The answer is the second attack on Israel/Jerusalem. This will then have them now all scattered. After the first attack the majority will still remain in the land and will believe at the decree that all is good. "Peace and safety". However, that is when the "Lion" of Daniel 7, the first beast, will attack. The first attack was not yet part of the "tribulation years", because it will occur before the 14 years. But this second one will be. It will be followed very soon after by the second beast of Daniel 7, the Bear. We can understand this from:

> ***Jeremiah 4:5-7*** *(KJV)*
> **5** Declare ye in Judah, and publish in Jerusalem;
> and say, Blow ye the trumpet in the land: cry, gather
> together, and say, Assemble yourselves, and let us
> go into the defenced cities.
> **6** Set up the standard toward Zion: retire, stay not:
> for I will bring evil **from the north**, and a great
> destruction.
> **7** **The lion** is come up from his thicket, and the
> destroyer of the Gentiles is on his way; he is gone

forth from his place to make thy land desolate; and thy cities shall be laid waste, without an inhabitant.

This is the lion coming from the North of Jerusalem to destroy it, in what it says will be, "a great destruction" and be left "without an inhabitant". The same destruction that will now remove them from the land for 7 years. This will have happened right around the time of the decree to rebuild. Many people do not understand that this lion is going to be Syria's leader, Assad. As a side note, there is some very interesting information about his family name. When his family took over in politics, the family's name meant beast! It was either his father or grandfather who realized it was not a good name to rule with, so he had it changed to Assad. Assad means, you guessed it...lion! Consider the evidence.

- from the North,
- hates Israel,
- last name was the beast and changed to,
- lion

Israel being weakened at the first attack, will easily be destroyed when Syria moves in to end it. And we find this in 2 Chronicles.

2 Chronicles 24:23-24 *(KJV)*
23 And it came to pass at the end of the year, that the host of Syria came up against him: and they came to Judah and Jerusalem, and destroyed all the princes of the people from among the people, and sent all the spoil of them unto the king of Damascus.

24 For the army of **the Syrians came with a small company of men**, and the LORD delivered a very great host into their hand, **because they had forsaken the LORD God of their fathers**. So they executed judgment against Joash.

This was allowed to happen to them even though Syria's army is small in comparison to Israel's, because the Jews/Jerusalem have forsaken the LORD GOD. We have also learned that they have forsaken God's law of rest for the land every 7th year, since having had the land of their fathers, Jerusalem.

WHAT WAS, SHALL BE AGAIN

In the book of Jeremiah we read about the second beast, the Bear, the destroyer of the Gentiles. This is the second beast of Daniel 7, and the Bear many would agree, will be Russia, who is a close ally with Syria. Going back to Revelation 6 what time would these two represent? The second seal. Let's see what it tells us when this horseman is released.

Revelation 6:3-4 *(KJV)*
3 And when he had opened the second seal, I heard the second beast say, Come and see.
4 And there went out another horse that was red: and power was given to him that sat thereon to **take peace from the earth**, and that they should **kill one another**: and there was given unto him a great sword.

We see that the "peace" that was decreed, was short lived. And as the peace is removed, the great sword is given that causes WW3, so that they begin to "kill one another". This is where we read in the discourses of Luke, Mark and Matthew that the tribulation begins on the whole earth. Here is Mark's version.

> ***Mark 13:8*** *(KJV)*
> **8** For **nation shall rise against nation**, and
> **kingdom against kingdom**: and there shall be
> earthquakes in divers places, and there shall be
> famines and troubles: these are the beginnings of
> sorrows.

What is incredible about what this says is that these things are only, "the **beginnings** of sorrows". We also notice in these beginnings of sorrows that it includes "famine". This falls in line with WW3 having broken out on the earth. Famine will most certainly soon follow. Also a great place to show how there is this overlapping that will happen between some of the seal judgments. WW3 will not have ended yet when the famine begins. The time of the Red Horse Rider, second seal judgment, WW3, will continue most likely for 2 to 3 years. Yet famine will not wait for it to end. It will happen during. Meaning that while the second seal is taking place, the third seal will begin it's portion. They continue together for a while. So now let us have a look at the third seal.

> ***Revelation 6:5-6*** *(KJV)*
> **5** And when he had opened the third seal, I heard
> the third beast say, Come and see. And I beheld,
> and lo a black horse; and he that sat on him had a
> pair of balances in his hand.
> **6** And I heard a voice in the midst of the four

beasts say, **<u>A measure of wheat for a penny, and three measures of barley for a penny</u>**; and see thou hurt not the oil and the wine.

We see that famine follows right on time according to scripture. How does this connect to Daniel 7's third beast, the Leopard? I do not believe it will be instant, as I just explained the famine will begin very shortly after WW3 breaks out. However, once things are in place, this famine period of time will be a time where food and all systems of the world will be controlled. As Daniel 7 says about this third beast, he will be given dominion (H7985) or control over the world systems.

dominion **(H7985)** from <u>H7981</u>; <u>empire</u>

H7981- have the mastery, have power, bear rule and to dominate, that is, govern.

This third beast, the Leopard from Daniel 7, I believe will be Germany that will also dominate with a small group of nations. Germany has been known for having excellent systems of control in history that were able to have control over whole countries. We only have to look back at WW1 and WW2!

All of it to this point is what we read in Mark 13 being only "the **beginning** of sorrows". What follows is going to be even more terrible, especially for Christians from this point forward to the end of the Seals judgments. This brings us to the fourth seal.

Revelation 6:7-8 *(KJV)*
7 And when he <u>had opened the fourth seal</u>, I heard the voice of the fourth beast say, Come and see.

8 And I looked, and behold a pale horse: and his name that sat on him was Death, and Hell followed with him. And power was given unto them over the fourth part of the earth, to kill with sword, and with hunger, and with death, and with the beasts of the earth.

We see here that this Pale Horse Rider being sent out has been given great authority to cause death over all the earth. Not only with the sword, but also famine, etc. Almost as if this one has the authority over the ones before it? Which would certainly have us thinking it lines up with the fourth beast in Daniel 7. Again not saying they are the same, but the timing of both would appear to be in line as to when their portion really comes into play. Remember, they were released closely together, but some were still building up until their time. Who is this fourth beast at this time in Daniel 7 that would bring us more or less to about the middle of the Seals judgments? Even though I would say it is more likely about 2.5 years into the Seals judgments.

At this point what we read in Mark 13 as the "beginning of sorrows", is coming to an end. It is the end of the "beginning of sorrow", which is in line with what we just read about the fourth seal by all its devastation. This is because this beast is the one now taking it all over. Let's read in Daniel again, because as mentioned, this is going to be a very important time.

Daniel 7:7 *(KJV)*
7 After this I saw in the night visions, and behold **a fourth beast**, ***dreadful and terrible***, and strong

> exceedingly; and it had great iron teeth: it devoured and brake in pieces, and **stamped the residue with the feet** of it: and it was diverse from all the beasts that were before it; **and it had ten horns**.

You are about to understand why this is now the time that will be even more "dreadful and terrible" than everything that had just taken place before it. Knowing from the chapter *"Who The Gospels Are Speaking To"*, you will understand this to be during Mark's group, the sleeping church time. There has also been great news during the first half of Seals, during this devastation. At this time of world war and devastation, it will also be the greatest time of revival in all human history! Just as September 11, 2001 caused millions and millions to return to church to seek the Lord, although not lasting more than 6 weeks. If that kind of devastation caused so many to go to church, how much more will WW3's devastation, famine, and all that will take place, cause them to truly come to the Lord and seek Him in forgiveness and repentance! This IS God's mercy in the midst of the Seals judgments. One final wake up call for the church that remains. What a devastating wake up call!

Let's look closely into this time period. First, if we go back and look into Mark 13 some more, we find this is the time where the fleeing into the wilderness is going to take place for **the church** that is now awake. And we find this here:

> ***Mark 13:14-19*** *(KJV)*
> **14** But when ye shall see **the abomination of**

desolation, spoken of by Daniel the prophet, standing where **it ought not**, (let him that readeth understand,) then let them that be in Judaea *flee to the mountains*:
15 And let him that is on the housetop not go down into the house, neither enter therein, to take anything out of his house:
16 And let him that is in the field not turn back again for to take up his garment.
17 But woe to them that are with child, and to them that give suck in those days!
18 And pray ye that your flight be not in the winter.
19 For in those days shall be affliction, such as was not from the beginning of the creation which God created unto this time, neither shall be.

This period is after all the devastation of WW3 and famine, during "the beginning of sorrows", that is now about to get much worse.

You will recall that we spoke earlier in the book how Mark had one "abomination of desolation" and Matthew had another? Well this is the time of Mark's, the sleeping church, "abomination of desolation" taking place. Right on time.

This fourth beast is better known as the "antichrist". We see his description in Daniel 7 having 10 horns and that he will "stamped the residue with the feet". If we go to the book of Revelation we find his description there:

***Revelation 13:1-2** (KJV)*
1 And I stood upon the sand of the sea, and saw a

beast rise up out of the sea, having seven heads
and **ten horns**, and upon his horns ten crowns, and
upon his heads the name of blasphemy.
2 And **the beast** which I saw was like unto **a**
leopard, and his feet were as the feet of **a bear**,
and his mouth as the mouth of **a lion**: and the
dragon gave him his power, and his seat, and great
authority.

We see the same description of the "ten horns" and understand he has been given power and authority over the three previous, the Lion, Bear and Leopard. As we continue we will see how long he is going to have this power for.

Revelation 13:4-8 *(KJV)*
4 And they worshipped the dragon which gave
power unto the beast: and they worshipped the
beast, saying, Who is like unto the beast? who is
able to make war with him?
5 And there was given unto him a mouth speaking
great things and blasphemies; and **power was**
given unto him to continue forty and two
months.
6 And he opened his mouth in blasphemy against
God, to blaspheme his name, and his tabernacle,
and them that dwell in heaven.
7 And *it was given unto him* ***to make war with***
***the saints*, and to overcome them**: and power was
given him over all kindreds, and tongues, and
nations.
8 And all that dwell upon the earth shall worship
him, *whose names are not written in the book of*

life of the Lamb slain from the foundation of the world.

I want to go to verse 7 before we get to the timing of it. We see here that he is going to be going after the "saints" and will be able to overcome them. Who are these saints? Believers in Jesus Christ of course! This is exactly in line with when Mark 13 tells them about the abomination of desolation now about to begin, and for the Christians to flee. GOD will lead them as they seek Him in prayer and they will not be left alone. There will also be workers for the Lord as mentioned, who will be helping them during this period as well, with safe places around the world in the wildernesses. However, we know not all will make it. Some will be captured and be given the choice to receive the mark of this beast at this time. Those who refuse to take it and not follow this beast leader or worship him, will be killed. He will not be alone when he comes to power at this time. There will also be another who will be like his "promoter", getting everyone to believe in this antichrist, and that everyone should take his mark and worship him. He will be able to do some pretty crazy wonders to get people to believe. This other one with him is known as the "false prophet". You will remember that we discussed this also in the chapter called "*The 40 days of the Son of Man*".

Revelation 13:11-18 *(KJV)*

11 And I beheld another beast coming up out of the earth; and he had two horns like a lamb, and he spake as a dragon.

12 And he exerciseth all the power of the first beast before him, and causeth the earth and them

which dwell therein **to worship the first beast**,
whose deadly wound was healed.
13 And he doeth great wonders, so that he maketh
fire come down from heaven on the earth in the
sight of men,
14 And deceiveth them that dwell on the earth by
the means of those miracles which he had power to
do in the sight of the beast; saying to them that
dwell on the earth, that they should make an image
to the beast, which had the wound by a sword, and
did live.
15 And he had power to give life unto the image
of the beast, that the image of the beast should
both speak, and **cause that as many as would not
worship the image of the beast should be killed**.
16 And he causeth all, both small and great, rich
and poor, free and bond, to receive a mark in their
right hand, or in their foreheads:
17 And **that no man might buy or sell**, save he
that had the mark, or the name of the beast, or the
number of his name.
18 Here is wisdom. Let him that hath
understanding count the number of the beast: for it
is the number of a man; and his number is Six
hundred threescore and six.

We can see how powerful this false prophet is going to be and will control all to the point that they will not be able to buy or sell. But whatever the cost, **DO NOT** take that mark, his name, number, nor worship him, even if it means death!

FEAR NOT, for if this is you during that time, you are mentioned in Revelation 6 at the **fifth** seal as to where you will be if you do not bow down to the beast. In Revelation 7 at the rapture and again in Revelation 20 when those who become martyrs are raised to live again, with Him for the 1000 years.

Revelation 6:9-11 *(KJV)*
9 And when he had opened the fifth seal, *I saw*
under the altar **the souls of them that were slain**
for the word of God, and for the testimony
which they held:
10 And they cried with a loud voice, saying, How
long, O Lord, holy and true, dost thou not judge
and avenge our blood on them that dwell on the
earth?
11 And white robes were given unto every one of
them; and it was said unto them, that they should
rest yet for a little season, until their fellow servants
also and their brethren, that should be killed as
they were, should be fulfilled.

And here they are after rapture in chapter 7.

Revelation 7:9 *(KJV)*
9 After this I beheld, and, lo, a great multitude, which no man could number, of all nations, and kindreds, and people, and tongues, *stood before the throne, and before the Lamb*, **clothed with white robes**, and palms in their hands;

We read here of his power that will last 42 months. There is another place that tells us a little more about what will be happening during this same time, directly in line with what we have just discussed. Unless you had the word definitions from the Strong's Concordance showing the Greek and Hebrew, as you have seen shared throughout the book, you would not think that it is saying to us what it is really saying. These definitions at our fingertips, with the online tools mentioned, are what help make the greatest difference in understanding and revealing so much more. This is one of those places.

Revelation 11:1-2 *(KJV)*
1 And there was given me a reed like unto a rod:
and the angel stood, saying, Rise, and measure the
temple **of God**, and the altar, and them that
worship therein.
2 But the **court (G833)** which is **without (G1855)**
the temple *leave out, and measure it not*; for it is
given unto the Gentiles: and the holy city shall they
tread under foot (G3961) ***forty and two
months.***

We can see that this is the same period of time of 42 months that was given to the beast/antichrist in Revelation 13, which is also the same wording from Daniel 7 about this beast and what he would be doing. He "stamped the residue with the feet", which means to trample. And here in verse 2 we read.

Tread under foot **(G3961) to trample** (literally or figuratively): - tread (down, under foot).

The same word only one is Hebrew and the other Greek.

So now we see that it is the same timing as when Christians are captured and are being killed. What then about this "court" or "temple of GOD to measure, and yet leave the outer part"? Let's start with the word meaning for "court".

Court (G833) by implication **a mansion**: - court, ([**sheep-]) fold**, hall, palace.

Remember, this is still the church age until the end of Seals. Where does the Lord dwell? He dwells in the body or the inside of a believer, which is the mansion. This will be until they are taken to paradise in the rapture to the place "prepared", as Jesus told us in John 14. We revealed this in the chapter *"When The Years Just Don't Add Up"*. And now let us look at the word "without" to seal this understanding.

Without **(G1855)** From G1854; external (-ly)

G1854 - away, forth, (with-) out (of, -ward), **strange**.

That is an interesting word for the meaning of "without". It turns out we can understand what this word "strange" can mean written in Jude 1:7... going after "strange **flesh**".

This scripture is telling us that this temple being measured is the spirit of those believers on the inside of their body/flesh, that is being trampled on by the enemy for 42 months.

Remember earlier I mentioned how I believed the first portion of sorrows would last about 2.5 years? Well, if you add it to the 42 months, you get to the end of the 6 years of Seals tribulation, and if we go to Revelation 6, what do we see at the end of it?

Revelation 6:12-17 *(KJV)*
12 And I beheld when he <u>had opened the sixth</u>
<u>seal</u>, and, lo, there was a great earthquake; and the
sun became black as sackcloth of hair, and the
moon became as blood;
13 And the stars of heaven fell unto the earth, even
as a fig tree casteth her untimely figs, when she is
shaken of a mighty wind.
14 And the heaven departed as a scroll when it is
rolled together; and every mountain and island
were moved out of their places.
15 And the kings of the earth, and the great men,
and the rich men, and the chief captains, and the
mighty men, and every bondman, and every free
man, hid themselves in the dens and in the rocks of
the mountains;
16 And <u>said to the mountains and rocks, Fall on us,</u>
<u>and hide us</u> **from the face of him that sitteth on**
the throne, <u>and from the wrath of the Lamb</u>:
17 <u>For the great day of his wrath is come; and who</u>
<u>shall be able to stand</u>?

At the end of the 6 years of Seals, also the end of the 6th seal, <u>we see that the Lord is coming down</u>, as we spoke about earlier in the book, as the time when <u>He will be coming down on Mount Zion</u>. Look at what we see happens in Daniel 7 after that fourth beast has had his time to reign.

Daniel 7:9-11 *(KJV)*
9 <u>I beheld till the thrones were cast down</u>, and **the**
Ancient of days did sit, whose garment was white
as snow, and the hair of his head like the pure wool:

his throne was like the fiery flame, and his wheels as burning fire.

10 A fiery stream issued and came forth from before him: thousand thousands ministered unto him, and ten thousand times ten thousand stood before him: the judgment was set, and the books were opened.

11 I beheld then because of the voice of the great words which the horn spake: I beheld even **till the beast was slain**, and his body destroyed, and given to the burning flame.

Just as at the end of the 6th seal, at the end of the 6th year, the LORD GOD shows up and **destroys that beast**. Jesus will be there too, as we read the time of His wrath is about to begin. When we spoke about this previously, we explained how His reign would begin after the final 7th year of Seals ended. That is because during that final year there are a few things happening. First off, let's finish off this portion that is so clearly connected to all this time of Seals from Daniel 7. After the *"Ancient of days"* who is GOD the Father is seen, we then read:

Daniel 7:13-14 *(KJV)*

13 I saw in the night visions, and, behold, **one like the Son of man came with the clouds of heaven, and came to the Ancient of days**, and they brought him near before him.

14 And **there was given him dominion, and glory, and a kingdom**, that all people, nations, and languages, should serve him: his dominion is an everlasting dominion, which shall not pass away, and his kingdom that which shall not be destroyed.

We see the Son of Man, Jesus, coming with the <u>cloud**s** of heaven</u>. This is all still that time at the end of the 6th year of Seals, shortly before the rapture will happen. We read in Mark 13 about Jesus who will come at this time, which by the way is not said in Luke's discourse. In Luke 21 He says "cloud", singular.

> ***Mark 13:24-27*** *(KJV)*
> **24** But in those days, <u>after **that tribulation**</u>, <u>the sun shall be darkened, and the moon shall not give her light</u>,
> **25** And <u>the stars of heaven shall fall</u>, and <u>the powers that are in heaven shall be shaken</u>.
> **26** And **then shall they see the Son of man <u>coming in the cloud"S"</u>** with great power and glory.
> **27** And then shall he send his angels, and shall gather together his elect from the four winds, from the uttermost part of the earth to the uttermost part of heaven.

Not only do we see Him here coming in the "clouds" as Daniel 7, but we also see events of the 6th seal with the sun and the moon and especially the stars of heaven falling.

Now that "that tribulation" has ended and the first 6 years are passed. Let's see what is going to be taking place during the 7th year of Seals. We can understand that approximately the first half of that year is what is told to us in Revelation 7. We see a group being chosen and sealed. This group is known as the 144,000 and their work is going to be during Trumpets judgment.

Following this group being sealed, the rapture of the great multitude take place. When we get to the 7th seal you see why I say it is about 6 months.

> ***Revelation 7:1-4*** *(KJV)*
> **1** And after these things I saw four angels standing
> on the four corners of the earth, holding the four
> winds of the earth, that the wind should not blow
> on the earth, nor on the sea, nor on any tree.
> **2** And I saw another angel ascending from the
> east, having the seal of the living God: and he cried
> with a loud voice to the four angels, to whom it was
> given to hurt the earth and the sea,
> **3** Saying, Hurt not the earth, neither the sea, nor
> the trees, **till** *we have sealed the servants of our*
> *God in their foreheads.*
> **4** And I heard the number of them which were
> sealed: and **there were sealed an hundred and**
> **forty and four thousand** of all the tribes of the
> children of Israel.

We can understand what is going to follow next by what the four winds are commanded not to do until this group is sealed. These four winds are going to be destroying parts of the earth, trees and sea. These are all associated with the events of the first four Trumpets judgments.

This 144,000 group as you will recall are the very same we see in Revelation 14:1 standing on "Mount Zion" with the Lamb. This is something many have questioned for a long time. How is it that the Lamb is on Mount Zion with the 144,000 about to be sent out to work? People have said that it must be in heaven and not on earth, because Jesus does not return until the end of tribulation feet down on the Mount of Olives. This thinking, as stated before, all comes because for generations the foundation of all teaching have come from Matthew's gospel. So it could never be properly understood that in fact it is the Lamb here on Mount Zion with them during this final year of Seals, before their work in Trumpets begins.

> ***Revelation 7:9-12*** *(KJV)*
> **9** After this I beheld, and, lo, ***a great multitude,***
> *which no man could number, of all nations, and*
> *kindreds, and people, and tongues,* **stood before**
> **the throne, and before the Lamb,** clothed with
> white robes, and palms in their hands;
> **10** And cried with a loud voice, saying, Salvation to
> our God which sitteth upon the throne, and unto
> the Lamb.
> **11** And all the angels stood round about the
> throne, and about the elders and the four beasts,
> and fell before the throne on their faces, and
> worshipped God,
> **12** Saying, Amen: Blessing, and glory, and wisdom,
> and thanksgiving, and honour, and power, and
> might, be unto our God for ever and ever. Amen.

Here we clearly see the rapture of the great multitude. As we know, Jesus has come down on Mount Zion as described earlier. What did He tell them in John 14, the exact chapter to year of John, that we shared in the previous chapter? Jesus told them He would go to "prepare" a place for them and that when He returned

He would **receive them unto Himself,** that where He was, so shall they be. If you recall, we shared that only in Mark's version when they went to make ready the Passover meal, were the words said, "... a large upper room furnished and "prepared": there make ready for us". - Mark 15: 14

And finally the Seals end with the 7th seal.

> ***Revelation 8:1*** *(KJV)*
> 1 And when he had opened the seventh seal, there was silence in heaven **about the space of half an hour**.

That is all of it. However, it leaves us with something that must be understood with a little more discernment. What is a "half an hour in heaven"? I believe it is pretty clear that we can understand this as a type and shadow of "about six months". By no means is this hard to really understand when we consider what has happened in chapter 7, which is the Lord coming down on Mount Zion at the end of the 6th Seal, the end of 6 years. This makes what happens in chapter 7 part of the 7th year, but it is before the 7th Seal, which indicates "half" of a time. I believe this is that time where the Lord will be making His covenant **with all people**, we spoke about previously.

This brings us to the end of Seals and the end of Mark's time, the Church Age. The end of the first 7 days/years after the Dove was sent the second time in Noah's story in Genesis 8:9. The end of the first 7 weeks/years of Daniel 9:25.

I would like to share with you an incredible piece of revelation before we jump into the Matthew portion of Trumpets judgment. It yet again brings more confirmation to these revelations. I am sharing it between the two, so you can have it in your thoughts as we move into the Trumpets.

All of this information shared thus far is a lot to take in. I believe what I am about to share will help you with what will happen in the future. We read of a Olivet discourse in all three the gospels of Luke, Mark and Matthew. The Olivet discourse is when Jesus was asked about what it was going to be like at the End Times, or at His coming. We know now that Luke's group, the Bride, is already gone before the 14 years begin. So we are going to look at Mark 13 and Matthew 24's Olivet discourse to show you this revelation. Of course none of the Olivet discourse is found in Luke, which is what we should expect, seeing that it is not applicable to the Bride.

In Mark's version we see no mention of "false Christs" or "false prophets", **BEFORE** he mentions the "abomination of desolation". It is only mentioned **AFTER** it. We read about this in Mark 13.

> ***Mark 13:22*** *(KJV)*
> **22** For **false Christs and false prophets** shall rise, and shall shew signs and wonders, to seduce, if it were possible, even the elect.

The antichrist and false prophet do not come truly onto the scene until he is given that power for 42 months as read in Revelation 13. Right at the time the first "abomination" of the mark of the beast comes. What do we know happens at the end of the 6th year/seal? The coming of the Ancient of days that destroys the antichrist, just as we read and covered in Daniel 7. It also told us that the Lord did not kill the others that ruled, but only took away their kingdoms and they lived a little longer. This means that the "false prophet" was not gone, only the antichrist, "false Christ". So now let's see how Matthew's version tells us the story.

We see in Matthew's Olivet discourse, that **BEFORE** the "abomination of desolation" is mentioned, that will happen to this group during Trumpets, only the "false prophets" is mentioned. No false Christs.

> ***Matthew 24:11*** *(KJV)*
> **11** And many **false prophets** shall rise, and shall deceive many.

Interesting, is it not? Especially knowing what you have come to understand about the gospels and their portions of time. Now we are going to look at "**AFTER** the abomination" in Matthew. Guess what we see written therein?

> ***Matthew 24:24*** *(KJV)*
> **24** For there shall arise **false Christs, and false prophets**, and shall shew great signs and wonders; insomuch that, if it were possible, they shall deceive the very elect.

Now all of the sudden it is "false Christs" and "false prophets" again? When would this timeframe equal in the End Time understanding? This is about mid-Trumpets when Messiah is "cut off", as shown in Daniel

9:26 or Zechariah 11, and other scriptures discussed. This is exactly when the 5th trumpet and first "Woe!" comes, when the pit is Opened!

To summarise, let's see what we have discovered.

- Second half of Seals, false Christ and false prophet show up
- End of the 6th seal/years only false Christ is killed, but false prophet gets to live.
- First half of Trumpets only false prophet on the scene
- Mid-Trumpets, at the opening of the pit and cutting off of Messiah, both false Christ and false prophet are there again.
- Until finally the Lord returns, once and for all feet down on the Mount of Olives and the antichrist and false prophet are cast into the lake of fire, first!

Not only was this proven in all the revealing of End Time scriptures, but it is also the answer to WHAT WAS, IS NOT AND SHALL BE

> ***Revelation 17:8*** *(KJV)*
> **8** <u>The beast that thou sawest</u> **was**, <u>and</u> **is not**; <u>and</u> **shall** <u>*ascend out of the bottomless pit*</u>, and go into perdition: and they that dwell on the earth shall wonder, whose names were not written in the book of life from the foundation of the world, when they behold the beast that was, and is not, and yet is.

He "WAS", is the 42 months, the second portion of seals, the "IS NOT" is the 1260 days of Messiah during the first half of Trumpets and the rebuilding of Jerusalem and the temple, and "SHALL", is when the pit is opened at the 5th trumpet, which is mid-Trumpets!

How incredible is it that we are now able to see and understand this! With the keys, as revealed in this book, you are able to make sense of it all and it all comes into view.

THE TRUMPETS JUDGMENT

At this point we now know and understand that the Lord has come down on Mount Zion. The mystery that remains of Him being on Mount Zion is what will it look like. I can only imagine what seeing something like that coming will be like! Where will it be and how? In the clouds over Jerusalem? I do not believe anyone can know that yet. So knowing this, let's have a look at what the scriptures do tell us about this time, through to the end of Trumpets.

Let's begin with some of the scriptures we have come to understand are speaking directly to this time of the 8th year of the 14, or the 1st year of Trumpets.

I have not shared this one in "*The Books Have Opened - chapters to years*", but it is another scripture to show you that this indeed is the understood time.

> ***Psalms 126:1-3*** *(KJV)*
> **1** When the LORD **turned again the captivity of**
> **Zion**, we were like them that dream.
> **2** Then was our mouth filled with laughter, and our
> tongue with singing: then said they among the
> heathen, The LORD hath done great things for

them.
3 The LORD hath done great things for us; whereof we are glad.

The Lord is bringing them back from their captivity to Him. We see how happy they are. This chapter of Psalms 126 is represented as the 8th year or 1st year of Trumpets on the *Tribulation Timeline Chart*, or the *Chapter to Year Graph*, found in the Appendix.

Zechariah 8:3-5 *(KJV)*
3 Thus saith the LORD; **I am returned unto Zion**, and **will dwell in the midst of Jerusalem**: and Jerusalem shall be called a city of truth; and ***the mountain of the LORD*** of hosts ***the holy mountain.***
4 Thus saith the LORD of hosts; There shall yet old men and old women dwell in the streets of Jerusalem, and every man with his staff in his hand for very age.
5 And the streets of the city shall be full of boys and girls playing in the streets thereof.

As you read the rest of Zechariah 8, it goes on to talk about rebuilding the temple and that it could not happen before this time.

Zechariah 8:9-10 *(KJV)*
9 Thus saith the LORD of hosts; Let your hands be strong, ye that hear in these days these words by the mouth of the prophets, which were in the day that the foundation of the house of the LORD of hosts was laid, **that the temple might be built**.
10 For before these days there was no hire for

man, nor any hire for beast; neither was there any peace to him that went out or came in *because of the affliction*: ***for I set all men every one against his neighbour.***

Just as we have read in Daniel 9:25-26, when the Messiah will be here and the rebuilding of the streets and wall will begin. There is however something I particularly want to share that will bring us back to the first few trumpets in Revelation. In Daniel 9:25 the verse ends with, "**even in troublous times**." We might say, how can it be in troublous times, when the Messiah is here and they are all happy to finally have returned to rebuild Jerusalem and the temple? The answer is in what is still happening around the earth as the time of trumpets begins. Let's not forget how Seals ended with not only a peace, but things were also still and quiet. That does not last long, because if you recall at the 7th seal, the angel had commanded the four winds to not yet blow on the earth with what they were about to begin. What were those things they were asked to hold back from doing for a little bit, "...he cried with a loud voice to the four angels, to whom it was given to hurt the earth and the sea, Saying, "Hurt not the earth, neither the sea, nor the trees, till..." This was at the start of the 7th year of Seals where there is still peace. During this period of peace they have been brought back into the land and this building is about to begin. The trumpet judgments are about to begin, which is the reason Daniel told us "even in troublous times".

Revelation 8: 6-12 *(KJV)*

6 And the seven angels which had the seven

trumpets prepared themselves to sound.
7 The first angel sounded, and there followed hail
and fire mingled with blood, and they were cast
upon ***the earth****: and the third part* ***of trees*** *was*
burnt up, and *all green grass was burnt up.*
8 And the second angel sounded, and as it were a
great mountain burning with fire was cast into the
sea: and *the third part* ***of the sea*** *became blood;*
9 And *the third part of the creatures which were* ***in***
the sea, and had life, died; and the third part of the
ships were destroyed.
10 And the third angel sounded, and there fell a
great star from heaven, burning as it were a lamp,
and it fell upon the third part of the rivers, and
upon the fountains of waters;
11 And the name of the star is called **Wormwood**:
and the third part of the waters became
wormwood; and many men died of the waters,
because they were made bitter.
12 And the fourth angel sounded, and the third
part of the sun was smitten, and the third part of
the moon, and the third part of the stars; so as the
third part of them was darkened, and the day shone
not for a third part of it, and the night likewise.

Just like the Seals, it is not one, one year, one the next year, but until completed. They "may" happen pretty close to each other in time. However, I do not believe they will. This total period of time for all four trumpets to happen is going to be 3.5 years. This will be the first half of the Trumpet judgments during which time Jerusalem is being rebuilt... even during troublous times.

When we look at these judgments we can see they were the ones held back until the group was sealed and Trumpets were to begin.

In fact for the third trumpet we see the star coming called "Wormwood". I believe in 2019, a well-known brother in Christ who travels the world giving talks and doing research about the scriptures, shared a vision he had that the Lord revealed to him that the coming comet, Apophis that was coming in 2029, was indeed the third trumpet star called Wormwood. Here is a little information about it.

"The closest known approach of **Apophis** comes on April 13, 2029, when **Apophis** will pass Earth **closer than geosynchronous communication satellites**, but will come no closer than 31,600 kilometres (19,600 mi) above Earth's surface"

That is seriously close and we can understand how the earth's gravity can pull it in being so close. Can we discern this to actually be Wormwood? Yes. I most certainly do believe we can and already have. The year 2029 is in the second year of Trumpets. Remember, they will happen over the 3.5 year period of the first half of Trumpets. This would be EXACTLY when it is coming. I personally do believe the Lord spoke to him and revealed it to him. I like to say it this way... "for the Bible told me so".

Let's face it, this is a whole lot of destruction happening on the earth in the first half of Trumpets. What about Jerusalem during all this? It is being protected by the LORD God as He said He would do. We read in Zechariah

2 that after Jerusalem had first been attacked and destroyed, there is someone referred to as a young man who goes, at what would appear to be about a year later in the understanding, to measure it all. But then we read an angel is told to go tell this man...

Zechariah 2:4-5 *(KJV)*

4 And said unto him, Run, speak to this young man, saying, Jerusalem shall be inhabited as towns without walls for the multitude of men and cattle therein:

5 For I, saith the LORD, ***will be unto her a wall of fire round about***, and will be the glory in the midst of her.

What else is taking place during this time? For one, the 144,000 have been sent out to evangelize with healing power and the ability to cast out demons and there is a battle in heaven that begins. Let's not forget the two witnesses protecting Jerusalem during this rebuilding time.

We know the end of Seals equals the end of Mark's time. It might also make sense to see if we can find something about this at the end of Mark's gospel. Just as the great commission at the end of each gospel is different, so too does it equal the group it is speaking to that will work next. At the end of Luke there were workers for Seals, who Jesus chose during the 40 days. So too does Mark reveal the next group that will work trumpets, the 144,000.

Mark 16:15-18 *(KJV)*

15 And he said unto them, Go ye into all the world,

and preach the gospel to every creature.
16 He that believeth and is baptized shall be saved;
but he that believeth not shall be damned.
17 And these signs shall follow them that believe;
In my name shall they cast out devils; they shall speak with new tongues;
18 They shall take up serpents; and if they drink any deadly thing, it shall not hurt them; they shall lay hands on the sick, and they shall recover.

In fact this reminds me of another scripture I would like to share with you to help understand these "worker" groups very clearly. Those chosen during the Lord's 40 days, working during the Seals tribulation, is the group represented as the Apostles who bring about the coming great revival, beginning early Seals. They are also referred to as the "**foundation**" layers. They lay the foundation spiritually for the temple of GOD during Seals, but around the midpoint there will also be a foundation laid for the new temple that will be built during the first half of Trumpets.

What is interesting is that during the 144,000's time, the "**walls**" are being rebuilt, just as we read in Daniel 9:25-26. Meaning they are representing the spiritual walls being built and the physical walls will be going up during their time as well.

Then there is still Matthew. We know the end of Matthew means the end of Trumpets, with a group that will be chosen from among them as we read at the end of Matthew. They are the ones who will go out during the 1000 year reign of Christ on earth, to teach the world the ways of the Lord. They will no longer preach, because the world will know that Christ has returned and rules from Jerusalem. This final group who are chosen are from the 12 tribes and they represent the **gates** by which people will enter into the kingdom.

Exactly how a building project works. Foundation first, then walls on top of them, and finally gates in the walls to allow people in! Scriptures in Revelation 21 literally confirm this all to us.

Revelation 21:12, 14, 17 *(KJV)*
12 And had a wall great and high, and **had twelve gates**, and at the gates twelve angels, and names written thereon, which are the names of **the twelve tribes** of the children of Israel:
14 And the wall of the city **had twelve foundations**, and in them the names of **the twelve apostles** of the Lamb.
17 And he measured **the wall** thereof, **an hundred and forty and four** cubits, according to the measure **of a man**, that is, of the angel.

This is the description of spiritual New Jerusalem coming down from heaven at the end of it all. Amazing!

For some reason it seems when some people read scripture they think because reading something and suddenly the next verse is something else, that the event must happen quickly. This is rarely the case. This is often how people have come to understand Revelation 12.

Revelation 12:7-9 *(KJV)*
7 And **there was war in heaven**: *Michael and his*

angels fought against the dragon; and the dragon fought and his angels,
8 And prevailed not; neither was their place found any more in heaven.
9 And **the great dragon was cast out**, that old serpent, called the Devil, and Satan, which deceiveth the whole world: ***he was cast out into the earth***, and his angels were cast out with him.

When reading this it sounds like a quick battle, but that is not the case. You may ask, "But is Michael not the most powerful angel?" Yes, he is, but that does not make it easy or quick. The fact is, this battle between the good and bad angels is going to last the first half of Trumpets for 1260 days. This is the period of time given to us in the verse before it.

Revelation 12:6 *(KJV)*
6 And the woman fled into the wilderness, where she hath a place prepared of God, that they should feed her there a thousand two hundred and threescore days.

We have come to understand that the first 5 verses in Revelation 12 is the time of Seals right up to the man child being born. This birth represents Jesus having returned on Mount Zion and finally, "her child **was caught up** to GOD and to His throne". Giving us the time period right up to the rapture of the great multitude, the "was caught up" group we have covered. Then we see this 1260 days clearly making it the first half of Trumpets. We also see this 1260 days in another place.

Revelation 11:3-7 *(KJV)*
3 And ***I will give power unto my two witnesses***,
and they shall prophesy ***a thousand two hundred***
and threescore days, clothed in sackcloth.
4 These are the two olive trees, and the two
candlesticks standing before the God of the earth.
5 And if any man will hurt them, fire proceedeth
out of their mouth, and devoureth their enemies:
and if any man will hurt them, he must in this
manner be killed.
6 These have power to shut heaven, that it rain not
in the days of their prophecy: and have power over
waters to turn them to blood, and to smite the
earth with all plagues, as often as they will.
7 And when they shall ***have finished their***
testimony, **the beast that ascendeth out of the**
bottomless pit shall ***make war*** against them, and
shall overcome them, and kill them.

This scripture gives us a lot of information. It confirms when the 1260 days will begin. If you recall, the verse before it was about the fact that for 42 months the trampling under foot would have been going on. Another confirmation that this 1260 days comes AFTER the 42 months. We are told the work the Two Witnesses are doing during this period of time is to prophesy. Meaning for the first half of Trumpets these two very powerful witnesses will be doing just that. Anyone who tries to prevent them will pay dearly for it.

Each of these situations or grouping of events are all taking place during the first half of Trumpets or the 1260 days, until the beast ascends out of the bottomless pit.

When is this beast going to come out of the bottomless pit? At about mid-Trumpets, once Satan has been cast down. Daniel 12 actually tells just a little about it, but it is enough to put fear into those reading it.

> ***Daniel 12:1*** *(KJV)*
> **1** And at that time shall Michael stand up, *the great prince which standeth for the children of thy people*: ***and there shall be a time of trouble, such as never was since there was a nation even to that same time***: and at that time thy people shall be delivered, every one that shall be found written in the book.

Here we read that Michael has won the war in heaven and satan has been cast down to the earth at what is being referred to as, the greatest time of trouble that EVER has been or will ever be! This is a very hard time to try and even imagine how terrible it is going to be. It is literally going to be Satan and his fallen angels.

There is a lot happening during this time and we are given quite a bit of information in scripture about it. Let's finish with what Revelation 12 has to say about it.

> ***Revelation 12:12-17*** *(KJV)*
> **12** Therefore rejoice, ye heavens, and ye that dwell in them. **Woe** to the inhabiters of the earth and of the sea! for **the devil is come down unto you**, having great wrath, because ***he knoweth that he hath but a short time***.
> **13** And when the dragon saw that he was cast unto the earth, he persecuted the woman which brought forth the man child.

14 And <u>to the woman were ***given two wings of a great eagle***</u>, that she might **<u>fly into the wilderness</u>**, into her place, where she is nourished for <u>a time, and times, and half a time</u>, from the face of the serpent.
15 And <u>the serpent cast out of his mouth **water as a flood** after the woman</u>, that he might cause her to be carried away of the flood.
16 And the earth helped the woman, and the earth opened her mouth, and swallowed up the flood which the dragon cast out of his mouth.
17 And the dragon was wroth with the woman, <u>and went **to make war** with the remnant of her seed</u>, which keep the commandments of God, and have the testimony of Jesus Christ.

The first thing we see is that those in heaven are rejoicing because Satan has FINALLY been cast out, but then we read they say "<u>WOE!</u>" to those on the earth. This "Woe!" at that time is the first "Woe!" and with three trumpets that remain.

Revelation 8:13 *(KJV)*
13 And I beheld, and heard an angel flying through the midst of heaven, saying with a loud voice, **<u>Woe, woe, woe</u>**<u>, to the inhabiters of the earth</u> by reason of the other voices of <u>*the **trumpet of the three angels**, which are yet to sound*</u>!

The first "Woe!" will be at the 5th Trumpet.

Revelation 11:1-2 *(KJV)*
1 And <u>the fifth angel sounded</u>, and I saw <u>a star fall from heaven unto the earth: and to him was given</u>

the key of the bottomless pit.
2 And ***he opened the bottomless pit***, and there arose a smoke out of the pit, as the smoke of a great furnace; and the sun and the air were darkened by reason of the smoke of the pit.

Terrible creatures will come out of the pit, like scorpions that will sting all the people except those sealed with GOD's seal on their foreheads. These that are sealed are the 144,000. Their work will not be finished after the first half of Trumpets, but they will be given more power by Jesus before He is "cut off" at that time. You see this explained to us in Luke 10. Remember, in Luke 1 he tells us he knew all things and he knew them in order. This means that we do find information about other groups in Luke as well, because of his understanding.

Luke 10:17-20 *(KJV)*
17 And the seventy returned again with joy, saying, Lord, even the devils are subject unto us through thy name.
18 *And he said unto them,* **I beheld Satan as lightning fall from heaven.**
19 Behold, ***I give unto you power to tread on serpents and scorpions***, and over all the power of the enemy: and nothing shall by any means hurt you.
20 Notwithstanding in this rejoice not, that the spirits are subject unto you; but rather rejoice, because your names are written in heaven.

The fact that satan is seen falling from heaven is confirming to us the timing. We then see that they are given power that will allow them to tread on serpents and "scorpions". This is exactly what we read happens at the fifth trumpet when the pit opens. Satan was cast to the earth and out of the pit came scorpions that will sting everyone except those with the seal of GOD. This group is told they will tread on the scorpions and not be hurt by them. These are the 144,000 being given great power before Jesus is "cut off" at this time.

This is the same time connected to Psalms 90:10 after the 10.5 year point when they will "fly away". Just as in Revelation 12:14 and Zechariah 11:10-11 where we are told that He will break the covenant He made with all people, and on that day it was broken. Verse 9 before this tells us those who will be left will eat each other's flesh! Just as Michael and all those in heaven said to the people remaining on earth, "Woe to you now!". Let's not forget this is also Daniel 9:26, the time that when Messiah gets "cut off", which is also the point of Revelation 12:15 when Satan will go after the woman, "with a flood". The same portion from Daniel 9:26 we covered in the Daniel 9 chapter earlier, when he says "and the end thereof shall be with a flood". All of this is at mid-Trumpets, fifth trumpet!

The last verse of Revelation 12 tells us satan was so wroth or angry, and because he could not get the woman, he went after the remnant of her seed to make war with them. We know who this group is and they cannot be killed. However, there will be two others who will be prophesying for 1260 days that will then have come to an end. We read in Revelation 11 that when they had finished, satan makes war with them and kills them.

> ***Revelation 11:7 (KJV)***
> **7** And when they shall ***have finished their testimony*****, the beast that ascendeth out of the bottomless pit** shall ***make war*** against them, and shall overcome them, and kill them.

Here again is one of those places where people have assumed they were killed right away. However, if that was the case why say "he war against them". If there would not be a period of war, it would have simply said, "and he killed them". So we are to understand there is a war for some period of time. We spoke about this from Daniel 9:26 as well. As we keep reading down Revelation 11, the Two Witnesses do get killed, but not until the end of the 6th trumpet or I should say about 3.5 days before the end of the 6th trumpet. In Revelation 12:12 we see that "his time was short". So how short of a time is it from making war with them at the fifth trumpet to the end of the sixth trumpet or second "Woe!"?

This answer should be quite clear for all who have read from the start of the book until now. This starting point of the war is mid-Trumpets, which we know equals about 10.5 years and leaves us a total of 3.5 years to the end of the 14 years. We have understood that it will last until the end of the sixth trumpet when they will be seen rising to their feet after the 3.5 days, and taken into heaven with a great earthquake following. It then tells us this is the end of the second "Woe!". We read the following in Daniel 12.

Daniel 12:7 *(KJV)*
7 And I heard the man clothed in linen, which was upon the waters of the river, when he held up his right hand and his left hand unto heaven, and sware by him that liveth for ever *that it shall be for* **a time, times, and an half**; and when he shall have accomplished to scatter the power of the holy people, *all these things shall* ***be finished***.

We covered how this reference of; time, times, and an half equals 2.5 years of the final 3.5 years of Trumpets. We see once this period of time is over, it tells us it will "be finished". This is what we are given in Revelation 10 as well, revealing how long this war will be.

Revelation 10:5-7 *(KJV)*
5 And the angel which I saw stand upon the sea and upon the earth lifted up his hand to heaven,
6 And sware by him that liveth for ever and ever, who created heaven, and the things that therein are, and the earth, and the things that therein are, and the sea, and the things which are therein, that there should be time no longer:
7 But in the days of the voice of the seventh angel, ***when he shall begin to sound***, the mystery of God should ***be finished***, as he hath declared to his servants the prophets.

The mystery is over at this point, because at the very beginning of the seventh trumpet, the world will see the Lord returning feet down on the Mount of Olives. This is that final "one week/year" from Daniel 9:27, which means satan's time of rule on earth and the length of the war he will make against the Two Witnesses will last 2.5 years.

Let's go into more detail of the 6th trumpet that we have only now touched on briefly. We know now that this war will end at the end of the 6th trumpet. What happens next will be terrible. A group of 200 million army of horsemen will be released to kill a third of man on the earth, and they being so wicked at this point, still do not repent.

> ***Revelation 9:13-17*** *(KJV)*
> **13** And the sixth angel sounded, and I heard a
> voice from the four horns of the golden altar which
> is before God,
> **14** Saying to the sixth angel which had the
> trumpet, Loose the four angels which are bound in
> the great river Euphrates.
> **15** And the four angels were loosed, which were
> prepared for an hour, and a day, and a month, and
> a year, **for to slay the third part of men.**
> **16** And the number of the army of the horsemen
> were *two hundred thousand thousand*: and I heard
> the number of them.
> **17** And thus I saw the horses in the vision, and
> them that sat on them, having breastplates of fire,
> and of jacinth, and brimstone: and the heads of the
> horses were as the heads of lions; and out of their
> mouths issued fire and smoke and brimstone.

Wow! To think at this point that there could be any that still survived. However as we get to Zechariah 14 we will see there certainly were.

Leaving only the final 7th trumpet.

Revelation 11:15-17 *(KJV)*
15 And the seventh angel sounded; and there were great voices in heaven, saying, ***The kingdoms of this world are become the kingdoms of our Lord, and of his Christ; and he shall reign for ever and ever.***
16 And the four and twenty elders, which sat before God on their seats, fell upon their faces, and worshipped God,
17 Saying, We give thee thanks, O Lord God Almighty, which art, and wast, and art to come; because thou hast taken to thee thy great power, and hast reigned.

You will recall that Jesus told them in Luke 17:24 that when He comes it will be as lightning from one end of the earth to the other, in His "day". He went on to speak about those things that would come **first** when He said in verse 25: "BUT FIRST". This point is all of those "but first" that have come to an end and this is now what He started His answer with -

Luke 17:24 *(KJV)*
24 For as the lightning, that lighteneth out of the one part under heaven, shineth unto the other part under heaven; ***so shall also the Son of man be in his day***.

In this final year we are told in Daniel 9:27 that Jesus will renew the covenant He had made with all people and then break it in that one day. In Zechariah 14 we are told what He will do to all those who came against Jerusalem.

Zechariah 14:4, 8-9, 12 *(KJV)*
4 And ***his feet shall stand in that day upon the
mount of Olives***, which is before Jerusalem on the
east, and the mount of Olives shall cleave in the
midst thereof toward the east and toward the west,
and there shall be a very great valley; and half of
the mountain shall remove toward the north, and
half of it toward the south.
8 And it shall be in that day, that living waters shall
go out from Jerusalem; half of them toward the
former sea, and half of them toward the hinder sea:
in summer and in winter shall it be.
9 And ***the LORD shall be king over all the earth***:
*in that day shall there be one LORD, and his name
one*.
12 And this shall be the plague wherewith the
LORD will smite **all the people that have fought
against Jerusalem**; Their flesh shall consume away
while they stand upon their feet, and their eyes
shall consume away in their holes, and their tongue
shall consume away in their mouth.

That is quite the finish! The Tribulation has ENDED. The 14 years are OVER!

The only thing remaining is to bring those back who had been protected in the wilderness until the end of the final 3.5 years of Trumpets or end of the 14 years. When that happens it will be the time of the Final Jubilee. This is where all the tribes will receive their inheritance.

Here is what Psalms 33 and and 133 have to tell us about this Jubilee year;

Psalms 33:8 *(KJV)*
8 Let **all the earth fear the LORD**: let **all the inhabitants of the world stand in awe** of him.

Psalms 133:1 *(KJV)*
1 Behold, how good and how pleasant it is **for brethren to dwell together in unity**!

They have received their promised inheritance of land and are now dwelling together in unity in the Jubilee, until the end of the world with the Lord!

Matthew 28:20 *(KJV)*
20 Teaching them to observe all things whatsoever I have commanded you: ***and, lo, I am with you alway, even unto the end of the world***. Amen.

Revealing Revelation as:

- 2.5 years "beginning of sorrows";
- 42 months antichrist and false prophet;
- Final year Seals;
- 1260 days Messiah on Mount Zion rebuilding during first 4 trumpets;
- Time, times, and an half of satan's rule at Messiah's "cut off" and the;
- Time, and times, and a half safe in the wilderness;
- Final year when the Lord returns feet down on the Mount of Olives;
- Jesus destroys all who came against Jerusalem.

= 14 years + Jubilee!

From Genesis to Revelation the Books Have Opened and Prophecy of the End Times Revealed.

GOD IS GOOD!

How amazing is it to understand that this book is revealing what the BOOK of all truth, the Bible, has given to us to understand for such a time as this, that is just about upon the world. If you are reading this and you have not yet given your life to Jesus Christ as your Lord and Savior, DO NOT DELAY, call out to Him, ask Him to forgive you your sins and turn from them. Then read the revelations of the next chapter and understand that now you need to be baptized in Jesus Chirst's name for the remission of sins and receive the Holy Spirit.

This is to be done whether you are reading this before or after it has all begun. Please do not delay.

I look forward to meeting you one day very soon, in the presence of our Lord and Saviour Jesus Christ.

GOD bless.

CHAPTER 9

SEEING OR ENTERING THE KINGDOM

At first glance one might be tempted to skip this chapter or even hasten through it. But I can promise you that you will see the gospel in a whole new revelation as to the Repentance, Baptism and being filled with the Holy Ghost. As I said before, there will be a great harvest once the tribulation of Seals have started, and those that will be going through the Seals judgment will have to clean their hands as we read in Psalm 24, purified with fire, which is the tribulation. The reality is also that there will be many that thought they were ready, being saved, but have not allowed the Holy Spirit to prepare them, being ignorant or either willfully disobedient to walking and living a sanctified life. In other words, they did not live holy lives, but compromised with the world and have not truly laid their lives down for Him. However, they will still need to have an understanding of this teaching, even if they have been saved for many years. The revelation of the water baptism, the way He intended, is crucial to our understanding.

We have all been taught that once we have given our lives to the Lord that our garments are spotless and clean. But are our garments clean and spotless? We need to understand in these final moments what we may individually be needing to be assured our garments are clean and bright, and that our robes are GORGEOUS! Should you be reading this before the tribulation has started, you can still be saved and be baptized in the Name of Jesus Christ, and be filled with the Holy Spirit. Also, please do not pass this chapter by because you feel you are already saved, and think that you will already have the necessary understanding. There is much more to this revelation. The time is very short.

Let's start with where it all begins, taking into account that there is very possibly someone that will read this and have no idea what it means to be saved. Saved from who or what?

YOU MUST BE BORN AGAIN

We read in John 3 about the interaction between Jesus and Nicodemus.

> ***John 3: 1- 4*** *(KJV)*
> **1** There was a man of the Pharisees, named Nicodemus, a ruler of the Jews:
> **2** The same came to Jesus by night, and said unto him, Rabbi, we know that thou art a teacher come from God: for no man can do these miracles that thou doest, except God be with him.
> **3** Jesus answered and said unto him, Verily, verily, I say unto thee, Except a man be born again, he cannot **see** the kingdom of God.

Firstly, Jesus is addressing the true need that Nicodemus has, which is he must be born again. You may ask, "How do I get born again? I cannot get back into my mother's womb!". And this is exactly what Nicodemus said.

4 Nicodemus saith unto him, How can a man be born when he is old? Can he enter the second time into his mother's womb, and be born?

We have to understand that God is Spirit and the truth is, so are we. We tend to think that we are a soul, who have a spirit and we live in a body. The reality is that we are spirit, who have a soul, that lives in a body. We are first and foremost spirit. So, having been born of the flesh, we now need to be born of the **Spirit.**

John 3: 6-8 *(KJV)*
6 That which is born of the flesh is flesh; and that which is born of the Spirit is spirit.
7 Marvel not that I said unto thee, Ye must be born again.
8 The wind bloweth where it listeth, and thou hearest the sound thereof, but canst not tell whence it cometh, and whither it goeth: so is every one that is born of the Spirit.

In verse 6 Jesus in a sense is saying, "Yes, you have been born of the flesh, but you still need to be born of the Spirit. Being born of the flesh is one thing, and being born of the Spirit is quite another". This is not something you can do, but something only the Spirit of God can do. You just have to agree with it. You must want to be born again. So the question is, "Why should you?" Some people are perfectly happy with where they are, but some are desperate for answers. I am guessing that you may very well be of the latter.

The Word of God says that we were ALL born in sin. It does not seem fair, however it does not change the reality. You only have to look at a toddler to know that nobody has to teach them to manipulate, throw tantrums, lie, steal or any sin really. It comes naturally. We sin. As we go through life we start to get good at it. There may even be someone out there that says, "Well, I'm a good person! I don't deserve to go to hell!". Well, let me ask you. Have you ever stolen something? Have you ever looked after a woman with lust? Have you ever lied in your life? Have you hated someone? The chances are good that you would say, "Yes, of course!" Now let me ask you something hypothetical.

If you were going out to buy something for your wife at the store, and you see that the light is turning yellow, but thought you would rather speed it up, ending up going over the red...would that be breaking a law? Of course it would. You would be guilty of a law that says that we are not to drive through a red light. Very simple. What if an officer saw you, caught up with you and started writing you a fine? Would it work to tell him anything else other than what he saw with his own two eyes? Would you not have to admit that you did take a chance, being caught "red-handed"?

The reality is that God has given us laws to abide by. They were made for our protection, the 10 Commandments written in Exodus 20. In fact, He shortened it for us. He summed it up in 2 commandments.

Matthew 22: 36-40 *(KJV)*
36 Master, which is the great commandment in the

law?
37 Jesus said unto him, Thou shalt love the Lord thy
God with all thy heart, and with all thy soul, and
with all thy mind.
38 This is the first and great commandment.
39 And the second is like unto it, Thou shalt love
thy neighbour as thyself.
40 On these two commandments hang all the law
and the prophets.

You can use simple logic to see how this would basically cover the 10 commandments we are all familiar with. Maybe you would say at this stage, "But I love God and I love my neighbors!"

Well, this may be true to your standards, but what are His standards? You see, Jesus said that if you only look at a woman with lust, you are an adulterer. If you hate someone, you are a murderer. We cannot ask God to meet our standards, He is God after all. We have to meet His. Because we have broken His law from birth, we have to answer for that sin. Just like you would then have to pay for that fine when you went through the red light. Somebody has to pay. You may think at this stage, "Why can He not give me a break?" Well, if God gave you a break, He would then have to give everyone a break. The Word says that He is a righteous judge. That means He is fair. He does not have favorites and He judges fairly. Let's read what 1 John 3 says about the law.

1 John 3:4 *(KJV)*
4 Whosoever committeth sin transgresseth also the law: for sin is the transgression of the law.

Now the Word says that there is a terrible punishment for sin.

Romans 6:23 *(KJV)*
23 For the wages of sin is death; but the gift of God is eternal life through Jesus Christ our Lord.

Did you see that...death! We know God keeps His word. This means if you break His laws, and we have now successfully concluded that you most definitely have had since birth, then your punishment is death! God is holy and He is pure and righteous. However, He says that He does not delight in the death of anyone.

2 Peter 3:9 *(KJV)*
9 The Lord is not slack concerning his promise, as some men count slackness; but is longsuffering to us-ward, not willing that any should perish, but that all should come to repentance.

There you have it. He does not want you to perish, but He wants you to come to repentance. However, just like any other judge, should you have to stand before one, would want more than just "sorry". Sorry is a good place to start, but that just will not cut it. And if a human judge would not be okay with that, why would the Almighty God, who is not only the judge, but the One whom you have transgressed against? David said the following when he repented.

Psalm 51: 4-5 *(KJV)*
4 Against thee, thee only, have I sinned, and done
this evil in thy sight: that thou mightest be justified
when thou speakest, and be clear when thou
judgest.
5 Behold, I was shapen in iniquity; and in sin did my
mother conceive me.

He says, I have sinned against **You**. That is the first acknowledgement we have to make. You have sinned against Him, and you stand guilty before Him, and because you are guilty, He would be justified in sentencing you to death, which is eternal damnation in hell forever. A lot of people think that to repent is to change our minds, but it is in fact making a 180 degree turn into the opposite direction of how you used to live. <u>It is not just changing your mind, it is changing your life</u>. In your sin you walked away from God, but when you repent you walk towards God. Jesus came to save us from our sin.

Repent is **G3340**, which means change your mind, change the inner man, to think differently.

When you repent, it means to change your mind, to ask God for forgiveness for your sins against Him and others. If you change your mind from doing something, will you be doing it? No, it speaks of a change of heart and actions.

God knew that you would never be able to make up for sinning against Him. What could you possibly do to make right the wrongs you have done to others and to

Him? Even though He said the wages of sin is death, He also said something else after that.

"... but the gift of God is eternal life through Jesus Christ our Lord!"

Picture this scenario if you will. You are standing in the court of law before the judge, ready to be sentenced on the basis of your guilt. You have indeed gone through the red light. But you have no way of paying that fine. But, the judge says to you, "I know you cannot pay this, so I will help you out. My son will pay your debt."

We have done much more against God than just driving through a red light. The Word says that we have all sinned.

At this juncture, I have to caution you about the "two-sided coin" of forgiveness. Jesus said that when we pray the "Our Father" that we must ask Him to forgive us, in the same way as we have forgiven those who have trespassed against us. He then also later spoke to His disciples after they asked Him how often they need to forgive, telling them 70 x 7, which basically means that there is no limit. Then He tells them this story of a ruler who had this man that owed him an extravagant amount of money. His men brought this man who owed him this great debt to him and when asked to pay, the man begged for mercy. He had no way of ever paying this debt. The ruler had pity on this man and told him that he is pardoned of this debt. Well, it did not take long for this very same man, in fact whilst he was leaving the ruler's house, to stop someone who owed him money, grabbed him by the neck and demanded that he pay him! This man forgot the great debt that he owed the ruler, that was pardoned. He did not show the same mercy that was given to him. In fact, he cast him into prison. This ruler did not take kindly to this when his men came to tell him about this. He confronted this unforgiving man and asked him whether he should not have also shown the same mercy than what he received. This story is written in Matthew 18. Let's read what his end was.

> ***Matthew 18: 34-35*** *(KJV)*
> **34** And his lord was wroth, and delivered him to the tormentors, till he should pay all that was due unto him.
> **35** So likewise shall my heavenly Father do also unto you, if ye from your hearts forgive not every one his brother their trespasses.

Your repentance and asking for forgiveness will simply fall on deaf ears. God will not hear you if you hold a grudge or are unforgiving towards another. It does not matter whether that person is an unbeliever. He says in His word, "be angry, but do not sin in your anger, and also do not let the sun go down on your anger" (Ephesians 4: 26). In Romans 12 He says that we must leave room for vengeance, because vengeance is His. With this I caution you to make sure that you have forgiven all. In Hebrews 12 we are told that we are to follow peace with all man and holiness, without which no man shall see the Lord.

Romans 3:23 *(KJV)*
23 For all have sinned, and come short of the glory of God

Now the debt we owe God is our life. Remember, the wages of sin is death. God, the Heavenly Father says, "I will pay your debt. I will send my Son to die on a cross for your sin. He will die in your place so that you may go free." However, you have to accept the price He paid, knowing that when He gave His life for your life so that you do not have to die, He also bought you with His Blood.

1 Corinthians 6:20 *(KJV)*
20 For ye are bought with a price: therefore glorify God in your body, and in your spirit, which are God's.

I would be giving you "half a gospel" if I did not give you all of it, which would not make it the gospel at all. So being bought with the price of His Blood, means that you cannot now anymore go out and do as you want. You now no longer belong to yourself. You are His. When you accept this price He paid for you, you in fact give your life to Him, to live for Him. A life for a life. With this Blood of His Son, He bought you. He is saying to you, "I want you to know that I bought you out of slavery to sin. Not that you would be My slave, but that you would be My son or daughter. I love you and I do not want sin to separate us, but it does. The only way to Me, is through My Son, so that when you stand before me, you will be washed, because I am holy." This is what repentance is, to embrace His death and to lay your life down and turn towards Him with your whole being.

A lot of people call this works, but when you repent, you are actually saying I am going to stop sinning. How is stopping to sin, works? If I stop something, that means I am not doing it.

> ***John 3:16*** *(KJV)*
> **16** For God so loved the world that he gave his only begotten Son, that whosoever believeth in him should not perish, but have everlasting life.

God loves you. He formed you in your mother's womb and has always desired a personal relationship with you. He wants you to be His son/daughter, and He wants to be your Father. A Real Father. He wants you to be with Him, but because He is holy, you too have to be holy. The question is, "How do I get saved?"

You have to, like David in Psalm 51, acknowledge your sin before God and you have to do this with your whole being. You cannot fool Him. He says that He knows the heart of man. You have to mean it and you have to believe it. This is something that will require faith from you for Him to hear you. He hears you on the basis of the sincerity of your heart and the faith that you place in the price His Son paid for your life. Then, He wants you to do what a newborn baby does. What do they do? They open their mouths!

> ***Romans 10: 9-10*** *(KJV)*
> **9** That if thou shalt <u>confess with thy mouth</u> the Lord Jesus, and shalt <u>believe in thine heart</u> that God hath

raised him from the dead, thou shalt be saved.
10 For with the heart man believeth unto righteousness; and with the mouth confession is made unto salvation.

You have to believe in your heart, but once you have accepted His salvation, you have to go tell those closest to you. There are many people who do not do this and it stifles their growth in the Lord. Just like a child that never learns to talk at the right age.

When we read further in John 3, Jesus tells something to Nicodemus that a lot of people miss. He said to Nicodemus that once he is born of the Spirit, he will **see** the Kingdom of God. But you do not just want to **see** the Kingdom of God, you want to **enter** the Kingdom of God by being born of the Spirit and of Water! Let's read what He says in verse 5 of John 3.

YOU MUST BE BAPTIZED

Let's first start with what does water baptism mean:

The word "baptism" comes from the Greek word, baptizo, **G907**

1. to dip repeatedly, to immerse, to submerge (of vessels sunk)
2. to cleanse by dipping or submerging, to wash, to make clean with water, to wash one's self, bathe
3. to overwhelm

I think you get the idea. No sprinkling, but submerging. The sprinkling of a child and calling it baptism is a Roman Catholic tradition that has no place within the topic we are discussing. This is simply because a baby cannot be born again by the Spirit, because that baby has to do this by believing, which it cannot. It is by grace, THROUGH faith that we are saved. Should you want to know whether sprinkling water would qualify, the answer is unequivocally, no. Jesus was not baptized as an infant, but He was baptized as a 30 year old man. He was baptized in the river Jordan, and the word said that He came up...up from where? From out of the water. We are called to follow Him.

Some people believe that water is not necessary and that we are only to be baptized with the Holy Spirit. During the days of Noah, the people were evil and wickedness abounded on this earth. What did God destroy the earth with? With water! He baptized the earth.

> ***1 Peter 3: 20-21*** *(KJV)*
> **20** Which sometime were disobedient, when once the longsuffering of God waited in the days of Noah, while the ark was a preparing, wherein few, that is, **eight souls were saved by water.**
> **21** The like figure whereunto even baptism doth also now save us (not the putting away of the filth of the flesh, **but the answer of a good conscience toward God**,) by the resurrection of Jesus Christ:

This is a picture of water baptism and God is using water to cleanse the earth.

Why would Jesus use such a strange practice to qualify us to **enter** into heaven? What is the meaning behind baptism?

We know that after Jesus died on the cross, His body was placed in a tomb. When you die physically, the next step is to place you in a grave. This grave is what is spoken of in Colossians and Romans as being spiritually circumcised. The Word says that when you are baptized, you are buried with Christ and in Christ. All this has to be done by faith. Now let's see the rest of the story in John 3.

> ***John 3:5*** *(KJV)*
> **5** Jesus answered, Verily, verily, I say unto thee, Except a man be born of water and of the Spirit, he cannot **enter** into the kingdom of God.

Did you see that? Not only do you have to be born of the Spirit, but you have to be born of water as well. Just like you were born of the flesh and water had to break, so you too, in the Spirit are born when you go through the water! And what water is this? Jesus was talking about being baptized. He is saying here that those who are only born of the Spirit, but were never baptized, will only **see** the Kingdom of God. This means that they will live in paradise. These are those who will be going through the Seals judgment of 6 years who will be RAPTURED in the 7th year of Rest as we have discussed in this book. This is the place He has prepared for you that we read in John 14. But, should you still have time and the tribulation has not started, you can **enter** His Kingdom if you are born again, and baptized in the

Name of Jesus Christ for the remission of sin. To enter His Kingdom is to enter into the third heaven. This is great news! Not only are you being washed with the Blood of His Son, but you are washed with water too!

When we enter the waters of baptism, we are proclaiming the gospel message, which is that Jesus died for our sins, was buried, and lives again. Baptism is identification of ourselves with Him.

> ***Romans 6: 3-4*** *(KJV)*
> **3** Know ye not, that so many of us as were baptized into Jesus Christ were baptized into his death?
> **4** Therefore we are buried with him by baptism into death: that like as Christ was raised up from the dead by the glory of the Father, even so we also should walk in newness of life.

If you believe that baptism in water is not really that important, this scripture shows you that there is no other way to be buried with Christ. When you go down into the water, it is like being buried. The old you, or the old man, is being buried under the water. So you being born by the Spirit is your first step. Being born of water, is your second. It is both a burial and a birth. When you come out of the water, a new man, like Jesus when He was raised from the dead, is risen! In this way you are identifying with His death, burial and resurrection. This is an open declaration to the world and to the forces of darkness that you are no longer the same man, and no longer belong to them, but to the One that bought you with His blood. Being raised up out of the water expresses our new life in Christ and our union with Him.

Romans 6: 1-2 *(KJV)*

1 What shall we say then? Shall we continue in sin, that grace may abound?

2 God forbid. How shall we, that are dead to sin, live any longer therein?

Romans 6: 6-8, 11 *(KJV)*

6 Knowing this, that our old man is crucified with him, **that the body of sin might be destroyed, that henceforth we should not serve sin**.

7 For he that is dead is freed from sin.

8 Now if we be dead with Christ, we believe that we shall also live with him:

11 Likewise reckon ye also yourselves to be dead indeed unto sin, but alive unto God through Jesus Christ our Lord.

This does not mean we are perfect and no longer sin. What it means is that SIN NO LONGER HAS DOMINION over us. Remember, He came to save you from your sin. Sin was your slave master, but He came and bought you with His Blood. You are now no longer under the control and dominion of sin, but under the grace of God. Listen to what it says in Hebrews 10.

Hebrews 10: 26-27 *(KJV)*

26 For if we sin wilfully after that we have received the knowledge of the truth, there remaineth no more sacrifice for sins,

27 But a certain fearful looking for of judgment and fiery indignation, which shall devour the adversaries.

This is not an occasional sin, but a continuous and habitual willful sin.

However, when we do this occasional sin, the Bible says that we have an Advocate with the Father.

> ***1 John 2:1*** *(KJV)*
> **1** My little children, these things write I unto you, that ye sin not. And if any man sin, we have an advocate with the Father, Jesus Christ the righteous.

This is not about the initial repentance. That repentance was in conjunction with the water baptism unto the remission of sin. This is for when you occasionally sin after that, and not habitual willful sin. Here we are told to **confess** our sin, not to repent, having already repented at the start of our new life in Him. This we read in 1 John.

> ***1 John 1:9*** *(KJV)*
> **9** If we **confess** our sins, he is faithful and just to forgive us our sins, and to cleanse us from all unrighteousness.

Once we have repented of our sins and have been baptized in water, we no longer have to repent, but now confess our sins, also to one another, and DIE DAILY. That is different to repentance. Now we walk by the Spirit and no longer by the flesh. Therefore we purify ourselves daily as we read in 1 John 3.

> ***1 John 3:3, 5-9 (KJV)***
> **3** And every man that hath this hope in him purifieth himself, even as he is pure.

This "purifieth" is **G53,** which means to make clean, purify self.

This is dying to self daily, our covenant with Christ when He gave His life for us through His death, burial and resurrection, and we now give our life daily to Him. So let's read further.

> **5** And ye know that he was manifested to take away our sins; and in him is no sin.

He was not manifested to forgive our sins, He was manifested to TAKE AWAY our sins!

Then it says something beautiful…"in Him is no sin." Are we not when we are baptized in Jesus Name being buried in His death and are we not in Him?

> **6** Whosoever abideth in him sinneth not:
> whosoever sinneth hath not seen him, neither
> known him.
> **7** Little children, let no man deceive you: he that
> doeth righteousness is righteous, even as he is
> righteous.
> **8 He that committeth sin is of the devil; for the**
> **devil sinneth from the beginning.**

For this purpose the Son of God was manifested, that he might destroy the works of the devil.

What! Do you see that? Remember, this is not talking about those occasional sins that we confess. This is specifically talking about those who willfully sin on a habitual basis. They are not of God, but of the devil. This is a very harsh word, especially if we think of how many Christians who say they are born again, keep on sinning without a care and do so habitually. God is not mocked. We read further -

> **9 <u>Whosoever is born of God doth not commit sin; for his seed remaineth in him: and he cannot sin, because he is born of God.</u>**

If we truly embrace Jesus' death, burial and resurrection and not just say we believe it, but have truly changed our ways, we will still have an occasional sin, but not willfully do it. However, if we are filled with the Spirit we will find that our life of sin will not be there anymore. It does not mean I will not make a mistake, but I am not living that life of sin anymore. I am united with His death, buried with Him in baptism and have received the gift of Holiness and Righteousness, which is the Holy Ghost.

In Acts 22 Paul was giving his testimony of what happened to him in Acts 9 at his conversion. The Lord gives Ananias instructions to go to Paul and lay his hands on him that he may receive his sight. Then Ananias tells him the following:

> ***Acts 22:16*** *(KJV)*
> **16** And now why tarriest thou? Arise, and be baptized, and wash away thy sins, calling on the name of the Lord.

We can receive the Holy Spirit without being baptized. Many people have experienced this. But God still requires the baptism of water for the remission of sin in the Name of Jesus Christ. Cornelius is an example, who was the first Gentile to receive the Holy Ghost. Peter was sitting on the roof and he received the vision of the sheet with all the unclean animals, which was God saying that He desires that ALL would come to salvation, which included the Gentiles. So then Peter says something profound in Acts 10.

Acts 10: 47-48 *(KJV)*
47 Can any man forbid water, that these should not be baptized, which have received the Holy Ghost as well as we?
48 And **he commanded them to be baptized in the name of the Lord.** Then prayed they him to tarry certain days.

HOW BAPTISM RELATES TO JESUS

1. It means we have turned from the old life of sin to a new life in Jesus Christ.
2. It means we are publicly identifying with the death, burial, and resurrection of Christ.
3. It means we are openly joining the ranks of those who believe in Christ.

In summary:

- As you are standing in the water = Your old man died on the cross through repentance
- Being lowered in the water = You become dead to sin
- As you are raised out of the water = You are raised up by the Holy Spirit, a new man.

IN WHOSE NAME?

In this section I would like to show you the revelation of whose name we are to be baptized in. Should you wonder, it does make a difference.

We find in Luke 3:3 how before Jesus came onto the scene, John the Baptist was baptizing people.

Luke 3: 3-6 *(KJV)*
3 And he came into all the country about Jordan,
preaching the baptism of repentance for the
remission of sins;
4 As it is written in the book of the words of Esaias
the prophet, saying, The voice of one crying in the
wilderness, Prepare ye the way of the Lord, make
his paths straight.
5 Every valley shall be filled, and every mountain
and hill shall be brought low; and the crooked shall
be made straight, and the rough ways shall be
made smooth;
6 And all flesh shall see the salvation of God.

This "seeing" of the salvation of God is speaking of the end of the 6th seal, where the Ancient of days and the Lamb of God will be coming down on Mount Zion. This is when they will **SEE** it. What was John doing to prepare them to see the salvation of God? He was calling everyone to repentance and to be baptized. Let's read what the Lord said of John the Baptist.

Luke 1: 76-79 *(KJV)*
76 And thou, child, shalt be called the prophet of
the Highest: for thou shalt go before the face of the

Lord to prepare his ways;
77 To <u>give knowledge of salvation</u> unto his people
by <u>the remission of their sins,</u>
78 Through the tender mercy of our God; whereby
the dayspring from on high hath visited us,
79 To give light to them that <u>sit in darkness</u> and in
<u>the shadow of death</u>, to guide our feet <u>into the way
of peace.</u>

We have to remember what happens during the tribulation of Seals, which is the gospel of MARK, rapture group.

Mark 13:12 *(KJV)*
12 Now the brother shall betray the brother to death, and the father the son; and children shall rise up against their parents, and shall cause them to be put to death.

The ministry of John the Baptist, which will be those chosen to work during this time, will not only be to call people to repentance and to be baptised, but also to turn the fathers and sons, mothers and daughters to each other and bring restitution. This is what will be required, among other things, of those who will be left behind, having to be purified with the fire of the tribulation, to prepare them for His coming on Mount Zion, and the rapture. We find however that John refused to baptize those who have not repented, and did not have the fruit worthy of repentance.

Luke 3: 7-8 *(KJV)*
7 Then said he to the multitude that came forth to be baptized of him, O generation of vipers, who

hath warned you to flee from the wrath to come?
8 Bring forth therefore fruits worthy of repentance,
and begin not to say within yourselves, We have
Abraham to our father: for I say unto you, That God
is able of these stones to raise up children unto
Abraham.

The reality is that if you get baptized without truly repenting, all you will really get is wet. WE HAVE TO HAVE REPENTANCE BEFORE WATER BAPTISM for the remission of sin.

When we repent of our sins, the Blood of Jesus covers our sin, and the robe we have on will have His blood on. It will not be white even though our sins are covered. We have to wash our robe to make it gorgeous white, with the water of baptism. This baptism with water is done in Jesus Christ's Name for the remission of sins.

What does the word "remission" mean? This is Strong's word **G859**, which means pardon, forgiveness, freedom and liberty. FORGIVENESS!

This is why when we are baptized the flesh is circumcised by faith and we no longer walk in sin. Jesus did not only come to forgive us of our sin, but destroy sin in our lives. If I have a stain on my robe, and I cover the stain with blood, would I still see the stain? No, I would not. It would be under the blood. When we repent, immediately and supernaturally the blood of Jesus is applied to your life. God can no longer see your sin. He atones for your sin. The blood cleanses us, but do we want the stains covered with blood left there, even spiritually? No. Although our sins are cleansed, we are still wearing the same garment. This is the baptism of repentance that John the Baptist preached. But Jesus comes to bring remission of sins, not just through repentance, but water baptism as well, by being buried with Christ. When we go in with our garment, with the blood stains, in the water of baptism, all stains are removed and we are made WHITE and CLEAN...all has been removed.

> ***John 5:14*** *(KJV)*
> **14** Afterward Jesus findeth him in the temple, and said unto him, Behold, thou art made whole: sin no more, lest a worse thing come unto thee.

This is the definition of repentance. Once you repent, you sin no more. When you do, a worse thing will come unto you. This is why people who have repented before and have sinned again, their state was worse than before.

Without the shed blood of Jesus, which is His grace, there is NO remission. There is no forgiveness. However, you need to see that it is not just repentance that is required, but also water baptism for the remission of sins. Remember what the water baptism stands for. It is your identification with the burial of Christ, which is the circumcision of the flesh. The difference between those who repent and do not get baptized and those who repent and get baptized, is that according to John 3, the one will only **see** the Kingdom of God, which means they will go to paradise, and the other will **enter** into the Kingdom of God, which is the third heaven. In that scripture a distinction was made by the Lord Himself to Nicodemus, saying clearly what the result of each will be. Let's read further about in whose name we are to be baptized in.

> ***Acts 2:38*** *(KJV)*
> **38** Then Peter said unto them, Repent, and be baptized every one of you in the name of Jesus Christ for the remission of sins, and ye shall receive the gift of the Holy Ghost.

I want you to consider the time period and the type and shadow that it is for us. This is right after Pentecost, which according to our understanding is right about when the Tribulation will start. So this would make this the beginning of Seals judgment, which is the Mark, Left Behind group. This baptism that we see next in Matthew 28 is different.

> ***Matthew 28:19*** *(KJV)*
> **19** Go ye therefore, and teach all nations, baptizing them **in the name of the Father, and of the Son, and of the Holy Ghost**:

But let's just first confirm why baptism in this period is so important.

When did the gospel of REPENT, BE BAPTIZED AND RECEIVE THE HOLY GHOST begin? At Pentecost! Jesus first had to die and be raised for this to be applicable. The gospel was being fulfilled and preached by these three different acts. REPENTANCE, BAPTISM, AND RECEIVING THE HOLY GHOST. But in whose name? In the Name of Jesus, and not in the name of the Father, the Son and the Holy Ghost.

You will NOT find the same wording in Luke or Mark of being baptized in the Name of the Father, Son and Holy Ghost. Remember, Acts is the time period of Mark, the Left Behind group, which speaks of being baptized ONLY in the Name of Jesus Christ for the remission of sins, but Matthew is written to the Jews. Once Jesus returns in **the end,** feet down on the Mount of Olives, it will then be in the Name of the Father, Son and the Holy Ghost. Because everybody has been taught from Matthew, they are adamant that this is the only way. Every time someone was baptized in the book of Acts it was in the Name of Jesus Christ for the remission of sin. This is why baptism is a type and shadow of being circumcised in the flesh. The sin nature dies within the burial into the water.

If there is one person synonymous to the word baptism, it is John the Baptist. John the Baptist is spoken of in Luke. We have to remember that Luke says in chapter 1 that he has perfect understanding and that he knows all things in order.

> ***Luke 3:7*** *(KJV)*
> **7** Then said he to the multitude that came forth to be baptized of him, O generation of vipers, who hath warned you to flee from the wrath to come?

He is preparing them all to repent before the wrath to come. What is this wrath to come?

This "wrath" to come **G3709** is exactly the same wrath that we read about in **Revelation 6: 16**, with exactly the same Strong's Concordance number.

> ***Revelation 6:16*** *(KJV)*
> **16** And said to the mountains and rocks, Fall on us, and hide us from the face of him that sitteth on the throne, and from the wrath of the Lamb:

Proving to us that this time period is at the end of the 6th seal when the Lamb of God shall return on Mount Zion with the Ancient of days. Just as John the Baptist began his ministry about 6 months before Jesus came to be baptized, so shall this end time John type and shadow prophet show up about 6 months before the end of the 6th year of the Seals judgment. He will restore families, before the rapture. As we read in Malachi

> ***Malachi 4:5-6*** *(KJV)*
> **5** Behold, I will send you Elijah the prophet before the coming of the great and dreadful day of the LORD:
> **6** And he shall turn the heart of the fathers to the children, and the heart of the children to their fathers, lest I come and smite the earth with a curse.

This is just as Jesus's ministry never truly or officially began until after John was beheaded. Almost exactly one year later. It shows us the exact same timing in the end. That one year later, the time of the 7th year Rest, is the time the 144,000 will be sealed, the rapture then happening and finally the 7th Seal of about 6 months. This will be before Christ having come on Mount Zion and officially begin His final 3.5 years of ministry during the first half of Trumpets.

Right after the outpouring of the Holy Spirit in the book of Acts, the people came to Peter and said, what must we do? To which he said in chapter 2:38

REPENT, and **BE BAPTIZED** everyone one of you in the **NAME OF JESUS CHRIST** for the remission of sin, and ye shall **RECEIVE THE GIFT** of the **HOLY GHOST.**

1. repent
2. be baptized
3. in the Name of **Jesus Christ**
4. Receive the gift of the Holy Ghost.

After you have been buried, you have to be raised out of the water, or the tomb, into new life, resurrection life. Jesus was raised by the power of the Holy Ghost. We see in Jesus' baptism, the heavens opened and John saw the Holy Spirit as a dove come upon Jesus.

RECEIVE THE HOLY SPIRIT

God does not leave us to our own to stop sinning and reckoning ourselves dead to sin as we read in **Romans 6**. He has promised to give us a Helper, the Holy Spirit. Jesus did not only come to forgive us our sins, but destroy it. We read in John 1 the following:

John 1:29-34 *(KJV)*
29 The next day John seeth Jesus coming unto him, and saith, **Behold the Lamb of God, which taketh away the sin of the world**.

30 This is he of whom I said, After me cometh a
man which is preferred before me: for he was
before me.
31 And I knew him not: but that he should be made
manifest to Israel, therefore am I come baptizing
with water.
32 And John bare record, saying, I saw the Spirit
descending from heaven like a dove, and it abode
upon him.
33 And I knew him not: but he that sent me to
baptize with water, the same said unto me, Upon
whom thou shalt see the Spirit descending, and
remaining on him, the same is he which baptizeth
with the Holy Ghost.
34 And I saw, and bare record that this is the Son of
God.

John said two things about Jesus:

1. He is coming to take away the sin of the world (verse 29)
2. He will baptize you with the Holy Ghost

John the Baptist did two things:

1. He preached repentance
2. Remission of sins through water baptism

For us, our acceptance is not only believing this, but we have to follow through with this. This is not a work. Jesus makes this clear right through the scriptures. If you want remission of sins, you need to repent and be baptized.

We read about Philip in Acts 8 that were baptizing people after they have repented.

Acts 8: 12-17 *(KJV)*
12 But when they believed Philip preaching the things concerning the kingdom of God, and the name of Jesus Christ, they were baptized, both men and women.
13 Then Simon himself believed also: and when he was baptized, he continued with Philip, and wondered, beholding the miracles and signs which were done.
14 Now when the apostles which were at Jerusalem heard that Samaria had received the word of God, they sent unto them Peter and John:
15 Who, when they were come down, prayed for them, that they might receive the Holy Ghost:

You have to understand, just because you believe, does not automatically mean that you have received the Holy Ghost. There are some that believed with repentance and did receive the Holy Ghost. But just because you believe it, does not mean you have received it. It has to be accompanied with repentance. They sent for the Apostles to come and pray for them.

16 (For as yet he was fallen upon none of them: only they were baptized **in the name of the Lord Jesus.**)
17 Then laid they their hands on them, and they received the Holy Ghost.

REPENT, BE BAPTIZED AND RECEIVE. IT CAN ALSO BE REPENT, RECEIVE, BE BAPTIZED. But none can be omitted.

> ***Acts 18: 24-26*** *(KJV)*
> **24** And a certain Jew named Apollos, born at Alexandria, an eloquent man, and mighty in the scriptures, came to Ephesus.
> **25** This man was instructed in the way of the Lord; and being fervent in the spirit, he spake and taught diligently the things of the Lord, knowing only the baptism of John.

This man was mighty in scriptures, fervent in the spirit, and spoke and taught the things of the Lord. This was a man of God. It says something interesting...**knowing ONLY of the baptism of John.**

Clearly letting us know that there is a big difference between the baptism of John and the baptism of Jesus. Remember, John said that Jesus will come and baptize with fire! When you read on, you will see that what it says in the next verse is exactly what we are doing here.

> **26** And he began to speak boldly in the synagogue: whom when Aquila and Priscilla had heard, they took him unto them, and expounded unto him the way of God more perfectly.

It is not that we know everything, but we are expounding more perfectly as the Lord reveals to us in His Word.

In Acts 19, Paul was in Ephesus where they were teaching John's baptism. As Paul was walking, he saw these men and knew that they were disciples. He asked them something very important.

Acts 19: 1-6 *(KJV)*
1 And it came to pass, that, while Apollos was at
Corinth, Paul having passed through the upper
coasts came to Ephesus: and finding certain
disciples,
2 He said unto them, **Have ye received the Holy
Ghost** since ye believed? And they said unto him,
We have not so much as heard whether there be
any Holy Ghost.
3 And he said unto them, Unto what then were ye
baptized? And they said, **Unto John's baptism**.
4 Then said Paul, John verily baptized with the
baptism of repentance, saying unto the people, that
they should believe on him which should come
after him, that is, on Christ Jesus.
5 When they heard this, they were **baptized in the
name of the Lord Jesus**.

So Paul first asks whether they have been baptized with the Holy Spirit and when they said they did not know anything about that, he took a step back and wanted to know what baptism they received, which was the baptism of John. This was Paul's answer as to why they have not, which means he knew that they had repented, but they needed to take it further.

6 And when Paul had laid his hands upon them, the
Holy Ghost came on them; and they spake with
tongues, and prophesied.

The whole basis of this chapter is not just the fact that we have to repent, receive the Holy Spirit and be baptized, but that we have to be baptized in **THE NAME OF JESUS CHRIST**.

This is what we are told to do. This is not what we as a ministry are saying, but the scriptures are commanding it. A man with the name of Justin Martyr in the Roman Catholic Church, in the 3rd Century, changed water baptism into the Name of the Father, Son and Holy Ghost as we read in Matthew 28, where the early Church only preached baptism in the Name of Jesus Christ. So the question is, "Who do we want to follow? Man or God?" We have a responsibility to be faithful to scripture. We are looking at what the Word is saying to us. But let's read a bit more about the infilling of the Holy Spirit.

> ***John 7: 37-39*** *(KJV)*
> **37** In the last day, that great day of the feast, Jesus stood and cried, saying, If any man thirst, let him come unto me, and drink.
> **38** He that believeth on me, as the scripture hath said, out of his belly shall flow rivers of living water.
> **39** (But this spake he of the Spirit, which they that believe on him should receive: for the Holy Ghost was not yet given; because that Jesus was not yet glorified.)

This is Jesus' promise to us that when we receive the Holy Spirit, it will not be like a dam or a well, but living water. It is a continual flow of the Holy Spirit within you. You sense this when others speak to you by the anointing as well as the authority with what they are speaking. So let's go to Luke 11 again.

> ***Luke 11: 10-13*** *(KJV)*
> **10** For every one that asketh receiveth; and he that seeketh findeth; and to him that knocketh it shall be opened.
> **11** If a son shall ask bread of any of you that is a father, will he give him a stone? or if he ask a fish, will he for a fish give him a serpent?
> **12** Or if he shall ask an egg, will he offer him a scorpion?
> **13** If ye then, being evil, know how to give good gifts unto your children: how much more shall your heavenly Father give the Holy Spirit to them that ask him?

Do not think that someone has to lay their hands on you to receive the Holy Ghost. He is saying that you must ask, believe and you will receive. It is good to have someone praying for you that is already filled with the Holy Ghost, but not necessary.

It is not what is spoken over you when you are baptized, but what is actually happening when you are baptized. It may be that many people will not have someone to baptize them. What matters is that you go under the water, because it is in the action that you are being buried with Christ and it is in the rising that you come up as a new man. Some may not have enough water to fill a tub or a river nearby, or pool, but if you can have enough water to make yourself completely wet, you have not been sprinkled, but baptized. God knows the sincerity of your heart and He knows that you are doing it in obedience in the Name of Jesus Christ for the remission of sins, having repented first. He knows the times that we are in. The Lord will fill you when you ask Him, and remember He is the baptizer, not man. Look to Him and believe, and when you obey, do it with all your heart.

> ***1 John 5: 7-9*** *(KJV)*
> **7** For there are three that bear record in heaven, the
> Father, the Word, and the Holy Ghost: and these
> three are one.
> **8** And there are three that bear witness in earth, the
> Spirit, and the water, and the blood: and these
> three agree in one.
> **9** If we receive the witness of men, the witness of
> God is greater: for this is the witness of God which
> he hath testified of his Son.

If we omit any of these three, is there still an agreement? Just like you cannot take away from the Father, the Son and the Holy Spirit, in the same way you cannot take away from the Spirit (infilling), the water (baptism) and the blood (repentance). They are one!

If there is anybody reading this and you have not yet given your life to God, now is the time to do so and to repent of all your sin. Read this chapter again if you must. It is important that you understand that it is not God who wants you to go to hell, it is the enemy. God has made a way through His Son, by dying on the cross for your sins, so that you may have a living relationship with Him and be free from sin. He says in His word that

He wants you to be where He is. Repent of your sins with a sincere heart, believe in His Son. Be baptized in the Name of Jesus Christ for the remission of your sins, and ask Him to fill you with His Holy Ghost and with fire. He will never leave or forsake you.

And should you be one of those who are here during the Seals judgment, know that you cannot take the mark of the beast, or worship him or have his name. You will have to die for your faith. Remember what Jesus told the thief on the cross next to Him. The thief asked Him to remember him, and Jesus hearing the man's cry for salvation, told him that on the same day, he will be with Him in paradise. Paul said to die is gain, because absence of the body is to be present with the Lord. In one instance your life will be taken, only for you to receive everlasting life with Him. Many prayers are before the Father for those who will be left behind, done not only through this ministry, but many family members and Christians all around this world. God will not ignore the prayers of the righteous. He has not forgotten you, although you may feel that way. He has purposed you to receive this book so that you may know that He has made a way for you, to prepare you and now to use you, if you will let Him.

May the grace of God be upon you and may you enter His Kingdom and if you are in the Seals judgment, may you see the Kingdom of God and be in paradise. Amen.

Proverbs 14: 26-27 *(KJV)*

26 In the fear of the Lord is strong confidence: and his
children shall have a place of refuge.
27 The fear of the Lord is a fountain of life, to depart
from the snares of death.

APPENDIX

#1

Barley Harvest

Firstfruits

Jesus Christ
Lamb Passover
1Cor 15:20-24
Levi 23:10
Firstfruits (H7225)

Main harvest

Them that slept
Mat 27:52

Corners & gleanings

Those few remaining who come to believe at the very end of this cycle.

#2

Wheat Harvest

Firstfruits

Bride of Christ (Luke)
Levi. 23:17
Firstfruits (H1061)
Rev 5:11-12

Main harvest

Church left behind (Mark)
Rev 7:9-17

Corners & gleanings

Those few towards the very end of the cycle when the Lord 7th year of Seals comes to an end.

#3

Garpe Harvest

Firstfruits

144,000 (John)
Rev 14:1

Main harvest

Judah/ Israelites (Matthew) that will return unto their Messiah at His coming feet down

Corners & gleanings

Those few towards the very end of the cycle when the Lord 7th year of Trumpets comes to an end.

Appendix 1: The 3 Harvests

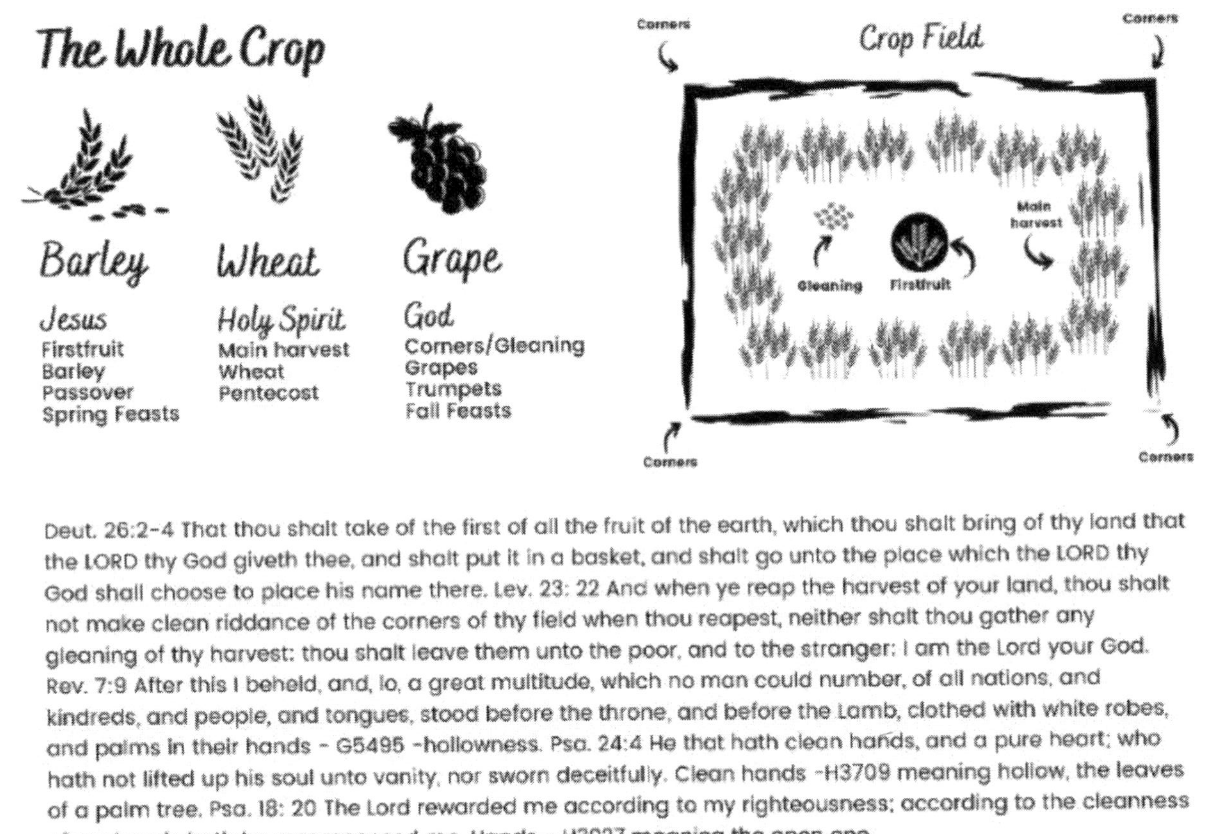

Appendix 2: The Whole Crop Field

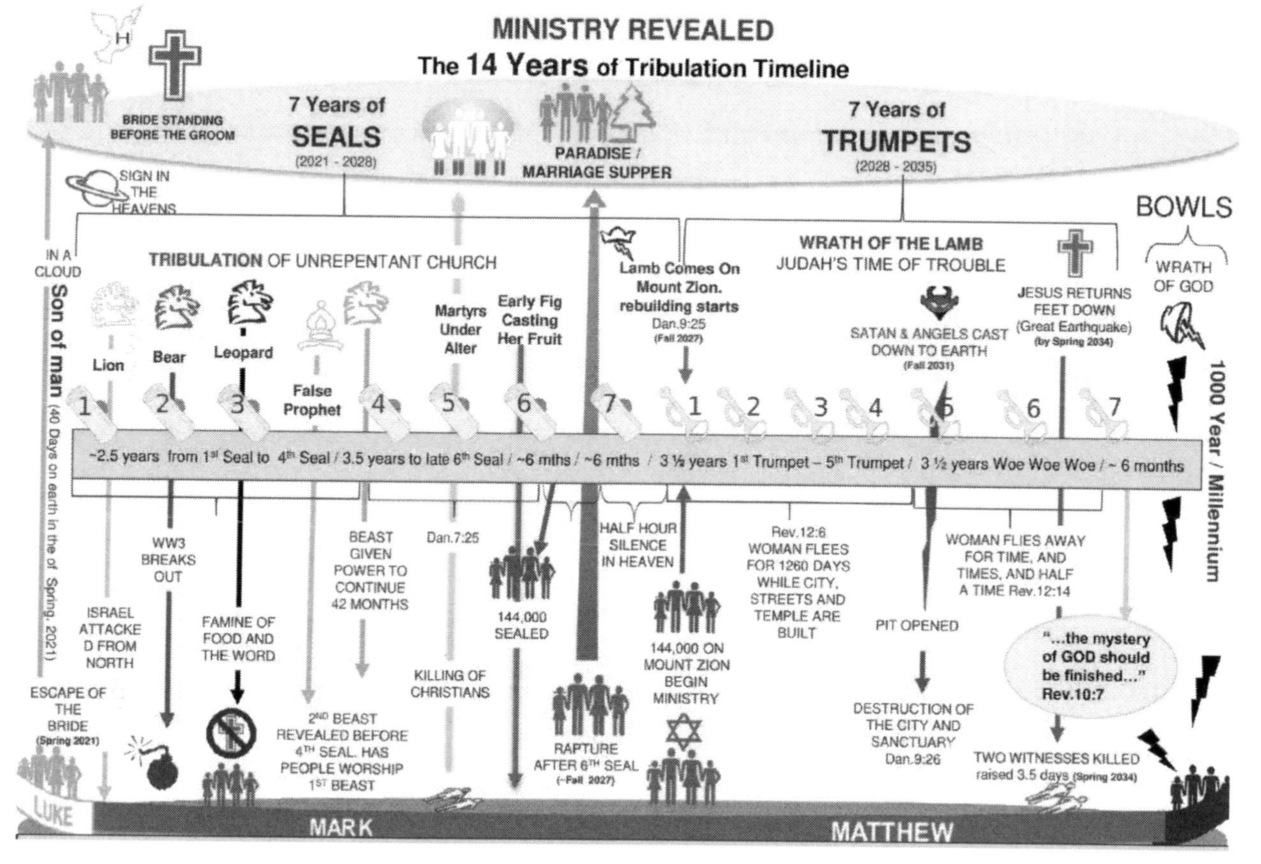

Appendix 3: The Timeline

	21	14	Tribulation		Hosea to Gentiles	Zechariah to Judah	John	Acts		Ezekiel	Psalms		Genesis	Hebrews	Exodus	Judges
	Year	Year		Year	Chapter	Chapter	Chapter	Chapter	Chapter	Chapter	Chapter	Chapter	Chapter	Chapter	Chapter	Chapter
Luke	1					Starts	1						1			21
	2					Fall	2						2			20
	3					2020	3						3			19
	4			Spring			4						4			18
	5			to			5						5			17
	6			Spring			6						6			16
	7		Sabbath	2020/21			7			33	18	118	7		34	15
Mark	8	1	Seals	2021/22	1	1	8	1	15	34	19	119	8	1	33	14
	9	2	Seals	2022/23	2	2	9	2	16	35	20	120	9	2	32	13
	10	3	Seals	2023/24	3	3	10	3	17	36	21	121	10	3	31	12
	11	4	Seals	2024/25	4	4	11	4	18	37	22	122	11	4	30	11
	12	5	Seals	2025/26	5	5	12	5	19	38	23	123	12	5	29	10
	13	6	Seals	2026/27	6	6	13	6	20	39	24	124	13	6	28	9
	14	7	Sabbath 7th Seal	2027/28	7	7	14	7	21	40	25	125	14	7	27	8
Matthew	15	8	Trumpets	2028/29	8	8	15	8	22	41	26	126	15	8	26	7
	16	9	Trumpets	2029/30	9	9	16	9	23	42	27	127	16	9	25	6
	17	10	Trumpets	2030/31	10	10	17	10	24	43	28	128	17	10	24	5
	18	11	Trumpets	2031/32	11	11	18	11	25	44	29	129	18	11	23	4
	19	12	Trumpets	2032/33	12	12	19	12	26	45	30	130	19	12	22	3
	20	13	Trumpets	2033/34	13	13	20	13	27	46	31	131	20	13	21	2
	21	14	Sabbath 7th Trumpet	2034/35	14	14	21	14	28	47	32	132	21		20	1
Year of Jubilee	22	15	Year of Jubilee	2035/36						48	33	133			19	

Appendix 4: The Chapters-to-Years

For a complete library of hundreds of free, 1-click downloadable videos of all Ministry Revealed in-depth teachings on the revelations contained in this book (and more), and many other resources, visit the Ministry Revealed website at:

www.ministryrevealed.com

REVELATION 22

1 And he shewed me a pure river of water of life, clear
as crystal, proceeding out of the throne of God and of
the Lamb.
2 In the midst of the street of it, and on either side of
the river, was there the tree of life, which bare twelve
manner of fruits, and yielded her fruit every month: and
the leaves of the tree were for the healing of the
nations.
3 And there shall be no more curse: but the throne of
God and of the Lamb shall be in it; and his servants
shall serve him:
4 And they shall see his face; and his name shall be in
their foreheads.
5 And there shall be no night there; and they need no
candle, neither light of the sun; for the Lord God giveth
them light: and they shall reign for ever and ever.
6 And he said unto me, These sayings are faithful and
true: and the Lord God of the holy prophets sent his
angel to shew unto his servants the things which must
shortly be done.
7 Behold, I come quickly: blessed is he that keepeth
the sayings of the prophecy of this book.
8 And I John saw these things, and heard them. And
when I had heard and seen, I fell down to worship
before the feet of the angel which shewed me these
things.
9 Then saith he unto me, See thou do it not: for I am
thy fellowservant, and of thy brethren the prophets,
and of them which keep the sayings of this book:

worship God.
10 And he saith unto me, Seal not the sayings of the
prophecy of this book: for the time is at hand.
11 He that is unjust, let him be unjust still: and he
which is filthy, let him be filthy still: and he that is
righteous, let him be righteous still: and he that is holy,
let him be holy still.
12 And, behold, I come quickly; and my reward is with
me, to give every man according as his work shall be.
13 I am Alpha and Omega, the beginning and the end,
the first and the last.
14 Blessed are they that do his commandments, that
they may have right to the tree of life, and may enter in
through the gates into the city.
15 For without are dogs, and sorcerers, and
whoremongers, and murderers, and idolaters, and
whosoever loveth and maketh a lie.
16 I Jesus have sent mine angel to testify unto you
these things in the churches. I am the root and the
offspring of David, and the bright and morning star.
17 And the Spirit and the bride say, Come. And let him
that heareth say, Come. And let him that is athirst
come. And whosoever will, let him take the water of life
freely.
18 For I testify unto every man that heareth the words
of the prophecy of this book, If any man shall add unto
these things, God shall add unto him the plagues that
are written in this book:
19 And if any man shall take away from the words of
the book of this prophecy, God shall take away his part
out of the book of life, and out of the holy city, and
from the things which are written in this book.

20 He which testifieth these things saith, Surely I come
quickly. Amen. Even so, come, Lord Jesus.
21 The grace of our Lord Jesus Christ be with you all.

Amen.

Printed in Great Britain
by Amazon